Advance Praise for
THE BBOOK OF GEEK

"As a lifelong geek, how have I made it this far without knowing
the eight pillars of geek knowledge? I was just a wandering geek
without any real guidance. You've put me on a more geekified
path and made me laugh in the process. Thank you, Brian!"

—Will Pearson, president, *Mental Floss*

"Briggs is the funniest guy on the Internet that most
people have never heard of. That's about to change."

—Drew Curtis, FARK.com

"My IQ went up twelve points just by reading this book."

—Sir John Hargrave, author of *Prank the Monkey*

THE BBOOK OF GEEK

BRIAN BRIGGS

CITADEL PRESS
Kensington Publishing Corp.
www.kensingtonbooks.com

CITADEL PRESS BOOKS are published by

Kensington Publishing Corp.
850 Third Avenue
New York, NY 10022

All Kensington titles, imprints, and distributed lines are available at special quantity discounts for bulk purchases for sales promotions, premiums, fund-raising, educational, or institutional use. Special book excerpts or customized printings can also be created to fit specific needs. For details, write or phone the office of the Kensington special sales manager: Kensington Publishing Corp., 850 Third Avenue, New York, NY 10022, attn: Special Sales Department; phone 1-800-221-2647.

CITADEL PRESS and the Citadel logo are Reg. U.S. Pat. & TM Off.

First printing: November 2008

10 9 8 7 6 5 4 3 2 1

Printed in the United States of America

Library of Congress Control Number: 2008932328

ISBN-13: 978-0-8065-3002-4
ISBN-10: 0-8065-3002-2

For Hedieh, Emily, and Michael

CONTENTS

INTERNET

INTRODUCTION

If you've gotten this far in the BBook, it proves that you can turn pages and have the ability to read. Those are the only two requirements needed for enjoying this BBook. You don't have to be a geek, but it won't hurt. Since we've already established your manual dexterity and literacy, let me tell you about this BBook in a way most comfortable for a geek like me: A list of frequently asked questions (FAQ).

The BBook of Geek FAQ

How could these questions be frequently asked when they were written before the BBook was released?

Using advanced time-traveling technology, I communicated with readers from the future to find out the questions they had about the BBook. Either that, or I made the whole thing up. Like many statements in this BBook, you'll have to choose what to believe.

What is a BBook?

The BBs come from the Web site this BBook evolved from: BBspot. In turn BBspot evolved from the author's initials, and his lack of foresight in coming up with a catchier name for his Web site. The time-traveling technology used to create this FAQ wasn't available in time to correct that.

What is a geek?

Now, *that's* a trickier question. Look around the Internet, which you've probably done in the past ten minutes, and you'll find different definitions, such as "a person interested in technology," or "someone passionate about a certain topic." Even the source of all knowledge, Wikipedia, doesn't have a clear definition.

I hate putting labels on people. For this BBook, I used what I believe to be the classical definitions. Geeks are defined by what they like, by what they take an interest in. I put those interests into eight categories: Software, Hardware, Internet, TV, Movies, Gaming, Literature, and Science. Passions in those areas define the geek world. These are the Eight Pillars of Geekdom.

I don't consider myself a geek. Should I still read this BBook?

Leading genetic researchers have determined that the geek gene can be activated at any time. It does not discriminate. There are only geeks and people who have not yet become geeks. Those same scientists say that *The BBook of Geek* best prepares you for that eventuality when it comes.

Should I read this BBook from beginning to end?

You can, but you don't have to. The BBook is broken into eight sections, each section has sixteen topics, and each topic has two pages dedicated to it. That's 2^8 pages of content for you to enjoy. You can access the pages randomly or systematically. You can employ the strategy of alternating between pages in the front and back until you finish in the middle. It's that user friendly.

How were the topics selected?

When the "pillars" were created, I and several other self-described geeks started compiling a giant list of potential topics. Narrowing down that mammoth list of topics to sixteen per category was a difficult process. Some topics were "no-brainers," like "Einstein" in the Science category, but others were much more difficult. Many topics could claim equal right to appearing in this BBook.

I did have a bias against newly geeky topics (sorry, *Heroes* fans). I wanted geek topics with a proven track record. I'm sure some personal bias snuck in as well. In the end a good cross-section of geeky topics has been selected.

My favorite movie/TV show/author/scientist/Web site wasn't included; are you some kind of idiot?

I think we can look to that font of knowledge known as the *Mystery Science Theater 3000* theme song for an answer to this question. And I paraphrase: "Repeat to yourself it's just a geek humor BBook, I should really just relax."

Why is Hitchhiker's Guide to the Galaxy *on page 42?*

Most likely you already know the answer to that question, but I'm using this contrived construct to let you know about some fun I had with the topics. I started with a chronological order for the topics, but I couldn't resist the geek urge to put certain topics on certain pages. I'll leave it as a fun exercise for the reader to find the other thirty-one specially-placed pages. I admit that some of the connections to the numbers are more tenuous than others, but they're there. (Hint: sometimes it's not just the page number, but the pair of page numbers for the topic.)

Speaking of page numbers, what the heck is up with pages like CF and 1A?

Don't be confused when you see pages numbered with letters. Since there are sixteen topics per category, it made the most sense to my geek mind (and probably yours, too) to number them in hexadecimal. Simple conversion tools can be found using "the Google," if you really need your pages numbered in decimal.

Did you know that your "facts" aren't really facts at all?

There's a saying that goes, "You can believe everything you read on the Internet." That's doubly true for this BBook. But, seriously though, BBspot is a geek humor site. We specialize in spreading misinformation to the masses. It's part of the fun. For even more fun, cite this BBook in your research papers and doctoral theses. It's a guaranteed A!

Where can I learn more about this wonderful world of geeks?

More fun can be had at the BBook's Web site, www.thebbookof geek.com and the site that inspired this BBook, www.bbspot.com.

SOFTWARE

Caffeine

Geek Cred: Caffeine fuels all-night programming and gaming sessions and it's not just for coffee and Cola anymore. There's caffeinated water, mints, and even doughnuts. If you need to stay wired, then caffeine is your drug of choice.

Geek Facts:

■ Caffeine in plants is a natural pesticide, often killing hungry bugs.

■ Caffeine is by far America's most popular drug.

■ International Decaffeinated Day, which encourages coffee drinkers to go decaf for one day a year, coincides with Global Homicide Day—serendipity?

■ Professional gamers have been known to rub caffeine gel on their mouse-clicking finger to gain an advantage.

■ For one project, Microsoft banned all programmers from ingesting caffeine to see if it would decrease programming errors. The resulting product? Windows ME.

■ Researchers have discovered that to deal with reindeer overpopulation, Santa Claus has begun feeding the reindeer caffeinated oats.

Office Jesus Turns Water into Coffee

LUFKIN, TX — The workers of Selby Communications are happy once again this morning, as their Office Jesus worked his miracles with the coffee machine.

Every morning for the past three years Jesus has been making coffee and sharing his words of wisdom with the people of Selby Communications. "Fellow workers, we have a mission today to get broadband services to my children of east Texas. Drink of this coffee, it is my blood. Eat of these bagels they are my body. Now go out there and sell, sell, sell!"

"The blood part kinda creeps me out," says coworker Avery McPhail, "but it's damn good coffee. I love his Sumatran-Mocha blend."

Before Jesus arrived, Selby Communications was a coffeeless company with only $2.3 million in sales. Now the coffee is flowing and they are approaching $78 million in revenue, all thanks to Jesus and the miracle of coffee. These facts haven't gone unnoticed by company executives, who promoted Jesus to VP of Coffee Making and Security.

President Henry Thomas said, "I think we hired him as a security guard originally. I saw him tinkering with the coffee machine one morning and told him that it hadn't worked for years. It would take a miracle for it to start working again. The next thing I know I've got a hot cup of Fair Trade Colombian blend, and I love it."

Selby Communications is a privately held company that sells broadband and wireless services in Texas and parts of Louisiana.

M. C. Escher

Geek Cred: Dutch artist
M. C. Escher is known for his
images of impossible con-
structions, like a hand drawing itself, or a waterfall that
feeds itself. Mathematicians
and scientists love Escher
because of his work with
symmetry and tessellations.

Geek Facts:

- The M. C. stands for
  Maurits Cornelis. His
  friends and family called him Mauk.

- Escher's largest print is "Metamorphosis III," which measures
  7.5' x 22.3'.

- Escher's least admired work was his 1965 print
  "Metamorphosis XII" of Elvis morphing into a fried chicken wing
  on velvet.

- Escher fared poorly in school and was forced to repeat classes.
  His guidance counselor famously said, "With grades like these,
  you'll never become a world-renowned artist of woodcuts and
  lithographs."

- Escher later drew that guidance counselor impossibly pulling his
  head out of his own ass.

- In 1984, Eschermania, a mental disorder that causes people to
  lose their minds after viewing Escher's impossible drawings,
  became a disease recognized by the American Psychological
  Association.

Valve Develops FPS Game with Escher Physics Engine

BELLEVUE, WA – Valve Software, makers of the popular Half-Life and Counter-Strike games, is developing a first-person shooter based on the drawings of M. C. Escher. The game, *Yes Sir, Escher,* will incorporate the Escher Physics Engine (EPE) developed by Valve.

Playing the role of a young artist trapped in the unique world of M. C. Escher drawings by an evil Dutch woodcut conglomerate, players will have to navigate through black-and-white levels like "Waterfalls" and "Hand with Globe". Most of the levels are impossible to finish—either they circle around on themselves or get smaller and smaller until they fade into nothingness.

Players will start with only a small knife, but will soon find some of the game's unique weapons. Erik Corter, who is heading up development of the game, said "One of the weapons will be the BFG or the 'Bird-Fish Gun.' Its bullets start out as birds, then turn into fish. The Escher-Illusion gun shoots bullets that hit the player in the back. It should make for some interesting game play."

He continued, "So far in our beta testing no player has been able to get past the first level, 'Waterfall', which isn't surprising since it's impossible to exit. It keeps going in an impossible circle. We may have to re-design that one."

Despite the impossibility of the game, players are eager to get their hands on it. "It'll be awesome to enter the world of M. C. Escher and blow it up," said one gamer.

Valve said the game will be ready to ship by the fall.

Richard Stallman

Geek Cred: Richard Stallman is a pioneer in free software. He started the GNU project, which led to the creation of GNU/Linux. He is also known for creating the ubiquitous Emacs text editor. He started the Free Software Foundation, which was created to support the free software movement.

Geek Facts:

- Originator of the GNU Public License (GPL), which is a software license applied to many free-as-in-freedom software projects.

- Created the original GCC (GNU Compiler Collection) which is the standard compiler that ships with Linux and other Unix-type operating systems.

- Always concerned with the power of language, Stallman legally changed his name to Richard Superman in 2005.

- Never concerned with material wealth, Stallman has not been able to afford a meal since 1972, and has survived on free coffee and doughnuts ever since.

- Stallman and Linus Torvalds settled their differences over the GNU/Linux naming convention with a sword battle at the 2004 California Renaissance Faire.

- Stallman created the GNU Pop Lock, a popular break dancing move seen in the movie *Krush Groove*.

Richard Stallman Changes Name to Recursive Acronym

BERKELEY, CA — In an unexpected move, Richard Stallman, creator of the Free Software Foundation, has legally changed his name to RMS, which he says stands for RMS's My Surname.

"I've been using RMS for years, so I figured I would make it official," said RMS. "And why not have a little fun with it?"

Recursive acronyms are acronyms that refer to themselves in the expanded acronym, thus creating an infinite loop. RMS has a long history with recursive acronyms. The GNU Project, which he started, helped along the free software movement as well as laying the groundwork for the Linux operating system. GNU is a recursive acronym that stands for GNU's Not Unix.

RMS said the name change should bring him more "street cred" among the next generation of geeks. "Creating a widely used compiler, text editor, debugger, and the General Public License just isn't enough these days. With a name like this, they'll have to respect me. Plus it should protect me from ninjas," said RMS.

RMS's announcement had other famously initialed individuals considering a move to match RMS's recursiveness. Eric Raymond, who often goes by esr, said he was planning on changing his name as well. "I was thinking of going with ESR's Strictly Recursive or ESR Skip Repeat, but can't decide."

Even others outside the geek community, like ODB and J. K. Rowling, were contemplating moves to recursive names, but no official announcements have been made.

One random Internet poster nicknamed linusforlife said, "Stallman, sorry, RMS, has really gone over the deep end this time. Next thing you know he'll be insisting everyone call it GNU/Linux."

This is the first time in recorded history a person has legally changed their name to a recursive acronym.

Bill Gates

Geed Cred: Bringing computing to the masses with MS-DOS and Windows made Bill Gates the richest geek in the world. Some geeks despise him for Microsoft's monopolistic business practices, and others question his skills as a programmer. However, with the glasses, the hair, and the centerfold poses with computer monitors, no one can deny his geekiness.

Geek Facts:

- Gates was arrested in New Mexico in 1977 for speeding and driving without a license.
- Gates also founded the digital imaging company Corbis to help add to his billions.
- Gates' daily workout regime includes a ten-mile run, an hour of free weights, and crushing the skulls of albino mice under the heels of his ostrich-leather cowboy boots.
- To counteract his philanthropic foundation, Bill Gates has started the Ultimate Evil Fund for financing truly evil projects around the world.
- Bill Gates and David Letterman buy their toupees from the same company.
- In 2003, Bill Gates and Bono arm wrestled to decide who helped Africa the most. Gates broke Bono's wrist in his victory.

Gates Says Linux Best OS Ever

REDMOND, WA — At a hastily convened press conference, Bill Gates announced that he personally thinks that "Linux is the best OS ever."

He added, "Ballmer is an idiot. The talk about how open source software damages intellectual property, or how Linux is a cancer, is moronic. When I heard these attacks I felt sick to my stomach. How could a company that I gave my life to spread these untruths? My conscience guides me, that's why I'm here today."

Gates talked for fifteen minutes, explaining why Linux was superior to all other computer operating systems—"especially Windows."

During the question-and-answer period that followed, many reporters openly questioned Gates's sanity and sobriety. "Have you gone mad?," "Are you drunk?," "What about Vista?" they asked. Though it was requested several times, Gates refused both a psychiatric examination and a breathalyzer test.

Dozens of Linux Web sites were quick to declare victory with headlines like "Torvalds Defeats Gates!" Others were more hesitant, and suspected a Microsoft conspiracy. Open source advocate Bruce Torman said, "Microsoft is at it again! Bashing . . . er . . . praising Linux. This argument that Linux is the best OS ever is just another red herring by the Microsoft PR machine. Aw, screw it, I don't know what the hell to make of it."

In addition to praising Linux as the best operating system ever, Gates also had some comments critical of Microsoft's flagship OS. "I never really liked Windows all that much," said Gates, "All that crashing and rebooting drove me nuts. I stopped using it about three years ago, but it was a pretty good moneymaker for the company, so we stuck with it."

Gates added, "Keep in mind that the opinions offered are my own personal opinions, and do not necessarily reflect the opinions of Microsoft."

A Microsoft marketing representative was heard muttering, "You got that right."

Linux

Geek Cred: The operating system of choice for geeks who value "free" in all its forms. An open source license means that anyone can modify and freely distribute the source code as long as their contributions are made available to the community. Linux is packaged in various distributions for use on various hardware platforms from mainframe computers to cell phones.

Geek Facts:

- The servers that power Google run on Linux.

- The idea for Tux the penguin, the Linux mascot, came from Torvalds after he was bitten by a penguin on a visit to Canberra, Australia.

- In 2000, the number of Linux distributions outnumbered the number of Linux users.

- Paris Hilton released Tinkerbell Linux, a distribution named after her dog and popular with Hollywood starlets.

- The proper way to pronounce Linux is to make it rhyme with "orange."

- The lack of games native to the Linux platform has forced many Linux users to rely on outdoor activities such as hiking and jai alai to satisfy their gaming urges.

Linux Developer Gets Laid

PHILADELPHIA, PA — In news that is sure to excite the Linux community, long-time Linux developer Todd Stanton got laid.

"I still have trouble believing it myself," said Todd. "I was doing some coding when my power supply blew. Rather than pulling out the spare like I usually would, I headed down to Best Buy to check out the new DVD releases. I bought another copy of *The Matrix,* since the one I had was pretty worn out. The checkout girl was a *Matrix* fan, too, and, well, one thing led to another."

Word spread rapidly on message boards and in IRC. "It's irresponsible of him and shows his lack of dedication to Linux and the free software movement," said Fred Simpson. "If others try to copy this behavior, then several projects could get derailed."

Others, like Gary Wilcox, were glad to hear the news, "We're tired of all those Microsoft developers shoving their Win-Hos in our face. Now we can tell them about Todd. Who's laughing now?"

Some developers are also excited that this may increase their chances of getting lucky, but most are being realistic. Walker Crandall said, "We thought we'd all be doing the hokey pokey after Bill Fitzsimmons got some during the LinuxWorld Conference in 1999. We were fooling ourselves. Nobody got nothing."

This is the third such instance for Linux developers since 1991.

Visicalc

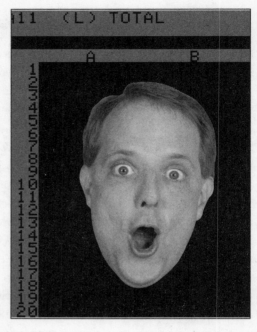

Geek Cred: The spreadsheet program Visicalc ushered in a new era in personal computing. Its release on the Apple II moved the computer from the home hobbyist to the world of business. The program was created by Dan Bricklin.

Geek Facts:

- At the time, software couldn't be patented, so Bricklin didn't profit from the explosion of other spreadsheet programs like Lotus 1-2-3 and Multiplan.
- The program was first sold in 1979.
- Visicalc contained the first "Easter egg" on the Apple II. If you put 666 in cell C66, then a laughing picture of Satan would appear.
- Bricklin conceived the idea for an electronic spreadsheet after watching a Tic-Tac-Toe tournament on ESPN.
- The first business use for Visicalc was to calculate the savings of firing two hundred accountants to be replaced by Visicalc.
- Rejected names for the program included Calcubator, Number Muncher, and I Can't Believe It's Not Tedious.

Spreadsheets Given Lifetime Achievement Award

SAN JOSE, CA – The Software Hall of Fame announced they were award-ing "spreadsheets" a lifetime achievement award for being the most boring software application, and presented the award at a ceremony last night.

Dan Bricklin, who created Visicalc, one of the first spreadsheet pro-grams, accepted the award on behalf of all spreadsheets. In his accept-ance speech, he said, "At the time, I thought people could do exciting things with spreadsheets, but right away they became the domain of ac-countants and other tedious number crunchers." Bricklin then droned on for another forty-five minutes to a mostly sleeping crowd.

Defragging applications and inventory management software were also considered by the panel, but the long history and wide adoption of spreadsheets clinched the victory.

"Visicalc may have helped usher in a new era of personal computing by bringing computers into the workplace, but the growth of spread-sheets sucked more fun out of computers than anything else," said one of the judges who wished to remain anonymous. "From sales forecasts to fantasy football leagues, wherever boring stats are, spreadsheets are there."

Evan Wilkinson, who presented the award at the ceremony, said, "From Lotus 1-2-3, Multiplan, Excel, and Google Spreadsheet, tabular formatted numbers with formulas bring the mundane to the masses. Even the occasional pie chart or brightly colored cells can't raise the needle on the excitement meter."

A permanent plaque will be placed at the Hall of Fame next to the Lifetime Achievement Award for the command prompt.

Programming Languages

Geek Cred: Most geeks at one point or another have done some programming. The first high-level programming language was FORTRAN, developed at IBM in 1957. Since then, hundreds of programming languages have been developed to handle different computing tasks.

print "Hello world!

Geek Facts:

- Programming predated computers, with punched paper scrolls for programming looms and player pianos in the nineteenth century.

- While most programming language use English words, many do not, including Phoenix, which uses Arabic.

- It's rumored that Bill Gates's first program was in BASIC and printed "Hello world, I'm going to take you over."

- Most of the delays in the release of Windows Vista were traced back to Microsoft's programmers still using punch cards to program.

- Sam Maxwell of Albany, New York, is the last living FORTRAN programmer.

- Most of the Linux kernel is programmed in Visual Logo with a touch of BASIC thrown in for stability.

Student Suspended for Suspected Use of PHP

TOPEKA, KS – Principal Clyde Thurlow suspended high school sophomore Brett Tyson after teachers learned he may be using PHP.

"He was immediately suspended as part of our Zero-Tolerance policy against drug use, no questions asked," said Thurlow. "We're not quite sure what PHP is, but we suspect it may be a derivative of PCP, or maybe a new designer drug like GHB."

Parents are frightened by the discovery of this new menace in their children's school, and are demanding something be done. "We heard that he found out about PHP on the Internet. There may even be a PHP Web ring operating on school grounds," said parent Carol Blessing. "School is supposed to be teaching our kids how to read and write. Not about dangerous drugs like PHP."

Interviews with students suggested that PHP use is widespread around the school, but is particularly concentrated in the geek population. Brett Tyson said, "I don't know what the hell is going on, dude, but this suspension gives me more time for playing games. Yee-haw!"

PHP is a hypertext preprocessor, which sounds dangerous. It is believed that many users started by using Perl and moved on to the more powerful PHP. For more information on how to recognize if your child may be using PHP, please visit www.php.net.

Vi vs. Emacs

Geek Cred: It doesn't get much geekier than arguing over which text editor stands above all. To defend the positions of the leading contenders, the Cult of vi and the Church of Emacs have been formed.

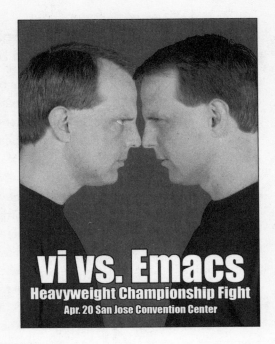

vi vs. Emacs
Heavyweight Championship Fight
Apr. 20 San Jose Convention Center

Geek Facts:

- Richard Stallman created Emacs. Bill Joy created vi. Both are preeminent geeks.

- Emacs contains a vi emulator mode, which could be considered an advantage or an admission that vi is better.

- Emacs only runs on iMacs.

- Richard Stallman famously said, "GNU/Linux isn't done until vi won't run."

- In the summer of 1983, ABC ran a television series called *Battle of the UNIX Editors.* According to Nielsen, three people watched the program.

- J. K. Rowling wrote *Harry Potter and the Philosopher's Stone* entirely on vi, and the rumor that she wrote it on a typewriter in a coffee shop is an urban legend.

Microsoft Ends Text Editor Debate,
Releases Notepad for Linux

REDMOND, WA — No geek debate except for possibly Kirk versus Picard has led to as many flame wars as vi versus Emacs, and it might be coming to a close as Microsoft plans to release Notepad for Linux.

"We're tired of all the casualties in the text editor war, and we thought we could end the bloodshed by releasing Notepad for Linux," said Microsoft's Envoy for Peace David Wu. "Too long Linux users have been tormented over which text editor to use. Their long free-software nightmare is now over."

Greg Martin, who lost a brother in the long-running war, was happy about the news. "I applaud Microsoft's move. Maybe this will be a step toward ending the epithets and jokes about macros. Not a day goes by when I think about how my brother was lost to the Mac because of all the insults."

Before the release, Linux users relied on emulators and dual-booting systems to get Notepad; now they won't have to any longer.

"Once Microsoft moves into an application space, they dominate," said Alvin Cromkin of the Gartner Group. "Vi and Emacs may be entrenched with Linux users, but it's hard to see them withstanding the muscle Microsoft can put behind Notepad."

Microsoft hopes that by getting Linux users comfortable with Microsoft products, they will be more likely to switch to Windows, but don't expect Microsoft to move other applications, like Word, to Linux. A Microsoft representative said that while they have a chance against vi and Emacs, it would be "difficult to compete with giants like OpenOffice.org, Kword, and Abiword."

Perl

Geek Cred: How can a programming language that's called the "duct tape of the internet" not be geeky? Perl was released into the wild by its creator, Larry Wall, in 1987. The book *Programming Perl,* published by O'Reilly with a camel on the cover, is the definitive reference manual for the language.

Geek Facts:

- The name comes from the Parable of the Pearl from the Book of Matthew.

- Perl is licensed under the GNU Public License (GPL) and the Artistic License.

- Three lines of obfuscated Perl code protects America's nuclear arsenal from accidental launch.

- Famed Perl hacker Thomas Grinnich recreated the retro-arcade hit Donkey Kong in only forty-two bytes of Perl code.

- His trusty Swiss Army Knife broken, MacGyver once used Perl to stop the assassin Murdoc from killing the U.S. Ambassador to Fiji.

- Perl hacker Bill Jenkins of Arkansas divorced his wife after she said that programming in PHP was "like visiting Nirvana compared to hacking in Perl."

Study Shows 99.99 Percent of High School Seniors Can't Read Perl

SAN FRANCISCO, CA – Recent results from the standardized Perl Fluency Test showed that 99.99 percent of U.S. high school seniors can't read Perl. This disturbing statistic shows that American students are painfully unprepared for life after graduation.

The four-hour test had two sections: a simple translation section and a project section. The first part asked students to translate easy Perl phrases into their standard English equivalent, and the second section required students to produce a simple MP3 player in Perl. "I didn't know what the hell any of it meant," said one senior, "it had lots of slashes and periods and brackets. It was so confusing. I'm feeling rather nauseous."

Perl experts were astounded by the results. "I was amazed that none of the students were able to read this simple sentence:

```
$_='while(read+STDIN,$_,2048 {$a=29;$c=142;if((@a=unx"C*",
$_) [20]&48) {$h=5;$_=unxb24,join"",@b=map {xB8,unxb8,chr
($_^$a[-$h+84])}} @ARGV;s/...$/1$&/;$d=unxV,xb25,$_;$b=73;
$e=256|(ord$b[4])<<9|ord$b[3];
```

"I mean, come on, that's so easy," said Paul Chen, chairman of the Learn Perl or Die Association, which administered the test nationwide. "Teachers need to start with simple phrases like $RF=~tr/A-Z/a-z/; and work up from there. We really need to start teaching this in first grade, if kids are ever going to understand this by high school."

Not everyone shared Mr. Chen's view about the necessity of adding Perl to early elementary curricula. Programmers Against Perl (PAP) spokesperson Keith Willingham said, "There's no better way to scare students away from computers than exposing them to Perl. Even experienced programmers are frightened and confused by it. The Perl lobby is just getting too powerful, and they need to be stopped."

Microsoft

Geek Cred: Started by a group of geeks, the company quickly grew to be one of the most important companies in computing. Its Windows operating system and Office suite dominate the market. While not as feared as it once was, Microsoft still holds great influence over the computing world.

Geek Facts:

- The first version of Windows was released in 1983.

- Microsoft was founded in Albuquerque, New Mexico, in 1975, and moved to Bellevue, Washington, in 1979.

- A flip of a coin decided the name of the company. Heads was Microsoft and tails was Uncle Billy's Code Farm.

- The original Windows 1.0 was very compact and contained only fifty lines of code.

- Steve Ballmer likes to write himself checks for $200 million, then go to Target to see if they'll cash them.

- Microsoft has outsourced several jobs to India because of India's lax laws regarding cybernetic implants on employees.

Microsoft Purchases Evil from Satan

REDMOND, WA – Microsoft purchased evil from Satan for $2.7 billion after many months of tough negotiations.

"We've been after Satan for some time," said CEO Steve Ballmer. "Negotiations were tough, but I think both Microsoft and the Prince of Darkness are happy with this deal."

Microsoft already controls 15 percent of the evil market, and with this purchase that number nears 100 percent. "We feel that there are real opportunities with evil, and that when evil is integrated into our next generation of Windows products, consumers will appreciate evil on their desktop," said Microsoft chairman Bill Gates. "Businesses haven't been able to fully realize their evil potential. With evil integrated into Office, corporations big and small will begin to see enhanced evil productivity."

"Evil is a real growing market," market strategist Frank Dresgan of Merrill Lynch explained. "Microsoft is a little late in the game, but even when they enter a market late they still tend to dominate. I think we'll see the same results with evil."

"I've been dealing with Microsoft for some time," Lucifer said. "I've been at this evil thing for millions of years, and wanted a way out. I considered an IPO, but then Steve-O and Billy came along and told me about their 'Evil Everywhere' plan. I just couldn't refuse."

Evil was founded by Satan close to the beginning of time. It has been growing steadily ever since, although most of the growth has accelerated with the development of the Internet. Satan plans to retire to a small island in the Bahamas and write a column for the local newspaper.

Bill Joy

Geek Cred: After receiving a degree in electrical engineering from the University of Michigan, he went on to be a cofounder of Sun Microsystems. He also created the text editor vi and the Java programming language. Not only that, he was largely responsible for Berkeley Unix (BSD) and SPARC microprocessors as well.

Geek Facts:

- In 2000 he wrote an article for *Wired* that outlined his fear of problems from advances in genetic engineering and nanotechnology.
- Much of Apple's OS X is based on BSD.
- A big fan of coffee, Bill Joy named his new programming language "Java" after consuming nothing more than coffee for six straight days.
- As creator of vi, BSD, and Java, Joy is no stranger to technology "wars." What most people don't know is that Joy also created Captain Kirk, KDE, and AMD.
- Known for his ability to multitask while programming, Joy coded most of BSD while playing the piano and simultaneously running a marathon.
- Joy married Marcia Pain in 1989. This was the inspiration for Rob Base's rap hit "Joy and Pain."

The Vatican Against Cloning
in Programming Languages

VATICAN CITY – The Vatican has announced today that all Catholic computer programmers must abstain from using cloning methods in Object Oriented programming, stating that the Church considers cloning an act against God. They have recently discovered that in most Object Oriented languages it is common for objects to be cloneable and possess a "clone()" method, which creates an exact copy of the object.

"We weren't aware that there are many programming languages that allow cloning," stated Giorgio Panzanella, a representative for the Vatican. "We are outraged that this cloning has been going on for quite some time now. God created those strings and linked lists. Who are we humans to clone them?

"The first language we found that allowed this sort of abomination was Java," continued Panzanella. "We have already issued an order to immediately excommunicate all of Sun Microsystems Catholic programmers. We also found out that programming languages for the .NET framework allow cloning, but Microsoft programmers have already sold their souls to Bill Gates and are already banned from the Church."

There have been reports of cloning gone bad. Antonio Miller, a Java programmer, admitted, "I was inexperienced, and I was trying to clone a JButton, so I made it cloneable. When I cloned it, however, the copy of the JButton was somehow merged with the original. They shared fonts, colors, and event listeners. The poor, wretched thing was suffering, so I had to garbage-collect it."

Sun has announced that it is considering replacing the Cloneable interface with a Copyable or Duplicateable interface in Java 1.5. Although the new Java Runtime Environment won't offer backward compatibility with current Java software, Sun hopes to get the Church off its back, stating that "we'd rather deal with email from angry programmers than cope with angry priests picketing outside the building."

Mosaic

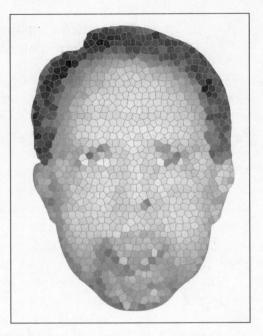

Geek Cred: Mosaic wasn't the first web browser, or even the first browser with the features it had, but the victors make the history. Developed at the National Center for Supercomputing Applications (NCSA) by Eric Bina and Marc Andreessen, it's the forebear of Netscape Navigator and Firefox.

Geek Facts:

- Andreessen left NCSA to form what became Netscape with Silicon Graphics founder Jim Clark.

- The first browser for the PC was Cello, created by Tom Bruce, but it made little impact.

- The code name for Mosaic during development was Operation EZpron.

- Mosaic was funded by a law proposed by Al Gore and Al contributed several sections of code, including the installation utility.

- The name "Mosaic" was chosen because Andreessen was having tile work done in his bathroom at the time.

- Mosaic's popularity can be traced to the fact that it was the first browser that allowed users to choose between amber on black or green on black for text colors, compared to just green on black for other browsers.

Top 11 Reasons Not to Upgrade to Internet Explorer 7.0

11. Because prime numbers are inherently evil.

10. Because by not using the browser, you'll keep Microsoft at only 94.56 percent of the browser market instead of 94.57 percent.

9. Because your pirated version of Windows won't let you install it.

8. Because some thirteen-year-old in IRC said that IE7 was "teh scuk."

7. Because you'll have a hard time finding the new IE icon on the desktop.

6. Because you've used Mosaic since the beginning, so why change now?

5. Because they don't make it for Linux.

4. Because your son will yell at you if you do an upgrade without his approval.

3. Because Microsoft hasn't made a good browser since Netscape Navigator 4.0.

2. Because the Mac nerds already have enough reasons to beat you up.

1. Because there are plenty of known bugs in IE6. No need to get new ones in IE7.

Photoshop

Geek Cred: Adobe Photoshop is the industry (and Internet) standard software for image editing. Just like Google, Photoshop has become a verb. Aimed at professionals, its high cost has led to many people pirating the software.

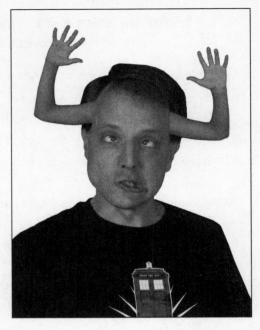

Geek Facts:

- Photoshop 1.0 was released exclusively for the Macintosh in 1990. It's now available for both Windows and Mac, but not natively for Linux.

- The program was first released under the name Barneyscan XP with Barneyscan scanners. No purple dinosaur included.

- Every year only one college student purchases a legal version of Photoshop. He's some rich kid at Harvard.

- Many conspiracy theorists believe that the moon landing was created in Photoshop.

- Adobe sued CBS News for using the term Photoshop as a verb in their newscast and won a $20,000,000 settlement.

- Never once has a user of The GIMP admitted that Photoshop is better.

Adobe Raising Pricing of Photoshop to Offset Losses to Piracy

SAN JOSE, CA — Adobe announced today that the company would be raising the price of their flagship Photoshop product to $9,995 to help counteract losses to piracy.

Adobe's vice president of sales, Leonard Idice, said, "It was a simple move to set the price. We just calculated our losses from piracy and priced the product to make up for it. I fully expect to sell the same number of copies."

One industry analyst thinks the move might result in lower sales. Carla Bellacruz from Bear Stearns said, "I'm not sure what they are thinking. Don't they know that most people are pirating it because it's too expensive? Now they go and raise the price by more than ten times? This is madness."

"No," said Idice, "this is Adobe."

Tom, a graphic artist who has pirated the software since version 3.0, said, "What's strange is that the new version doesn't even have any new features except for a new name and price. I believe this will only increase their losses to piracy. I mean, before I was just pirating an $800 program, now I'm pirating a $10,000 program. I might even pirate two copies!"

In response to the move, Bob Bobbin, who heads the open source project for The GIMP, a free alternative to Photoshop, said, "We're going to make our product even freer than it was before. People will definitely use us then."

Artificial Intelligence

Geek Cred: In science fiction, artificial intelligence applies to computer systems becoming self-aware and killing everyone on the space ship. In reality, it's about computers being able to perform tasks intelligently. In geek fantasy, it's never having to interact with a stupid human again.

Geek Facts:

- The term "artificial intelligence" was coined by John McCarthy in 1955.
- The Loebner Prize is awarded to the most humanlike computer based on a Turing Test.
- In 2006, artificially intelligent chatbots surpassed middle-aged men in impersonating teenage girls on the Internet.
- Chuck Norris beat Honda's humanoid robot "Asimo" in a karate match at an exhibition in Tokyo in 2005.
- Despite Hollywood's obsession with intelligent computers battling with humanity, scientists are unanimous in saying that it can't happen until 2010.
- In 2001, AOL became the first company to have a computer as CEO.

Bungie Dumps AI for Cheap Human Intelligence in Halo 3

REDMOND, WA – Dissatisfied with the artificial intelligence (AI) engine in Halo 3, developers at Bungie Studios have decided to outsource the game's AI for cheap offshore human intelligence.

"We just couldn't get the AI where we wanted it," said Bungie lead developer Kenneth Malek. "We decided it would be cheaper to hire real people to play the Covenant in the game, instead of paying expensive programmers to redo the AI. It'll be a unique gaming experience for everyone involved."

To cope with the massive amount of NPCs needed, Bungie will recruit players from all over the world. "We'll have people from India, China, Bangladesh, just about everywhere there's poor people," said Malek. "We figure with eight million people working eighteen-hour shifts, we can satisfy our needs."

Malek also explained that while the story line will remain the same, introducing human intelligence into the game will give it infinite replayability. "One time the best enemy character you face may be controlled by Habibul Ashraful from Bangladesh, who only has three fingers, and the next time it may be Li Ming, who farms gold in World of Warcraft."

Gamers were intrigued by the possibilities of gaming against other humans in a non-PvP environment. Fernando Hoobler from Omaha, Nebraska said, "This will be kick-ass. Not only will I be destroying the Covenant, but I'll be virtually blowing up foreigners, too."

Because of the change, players will need an Internet connection to play the stand-alone version of the game. Also, the change will delay the release of the game until October 28, but a Bungie representative said, "the wait will be worth it."

BitTorrent

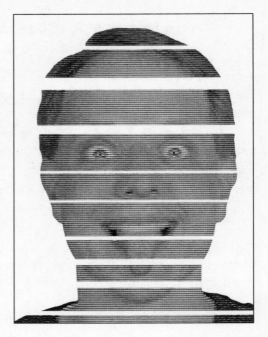

Geek Cred: If a geek wants the latest episode of a TV show or a new movie, BitTorrent is the solution. BitTorrent is a peer-to-peer file sharing protocol created by Bram Cohen. The BitTorrent protocol allows for distributed file sharing. A large portion of traffic on the Internet is from BitTorrent uploads and downloads.

Geek Facts:

- The protocol was released in July 2001.
- Sites that allow people to find illegal torrents of movies have been sued many times by governments and copyright holders.
- In its history, only three files have been legally downloaded using BitTorrent. The rest are all violations of copyright, according to the MPAA.
- A 2005 study by the Gartner Group showed that if all the bandwidth used by BitTorrent clients were stopped, the Internet would disappear in a puff of logic from lack of use.
- The first file downloaded using BitTorrent was the 1982 series finale of *Barney Miller.*
- Four out of every five terrorist attacks are financed by files downloaded using the BitTorrent protocol.

Top 11 BitTorrent Search Sites to Avoid

11. NeverEndingTorrent.com–500 petabyte zip files of random numbers

10. XenuTorrents.com–Only torrents approved by Tom Cruise.

9. Carrotorrent.co.uk–searches bootleg performances by prop comedian Carrot Top done in a British accent.

8. DefinitelyNotRIAATorrents.com–Nobody is tracking you here. Nope. Not at all.

7. TorrentsRUs.com–For kids, by kids, because kids can't go to jail.

6. Torgorent–Only versions of *Manos: The Hands of Fate* seeded.

5. Faketorrents.tk–All the file titles you ever wanted, without the actual files.

4. EmptyTorrents.com–The safest torrents on the net

3. EbaumsTorrents.com–Torrents from other sites, but the file name contains the words "Property Of EbaumsTorrents.com"

2. Farktorrents.fk–The file may be crap, but some of the comments are funny

1. torrents.goatse.cx–All of our torrent files have a big hole in them.

Firefox

Geek Cred: The browser of choice for a majority of geeks (at least for those who have accepted pictures as a part of Web browsing and jumped from Lynx). Firefox is the browser component of the open source Mozilla project that emerged from Netscape.

Geek Facts:

- First called Phoenix, then Firebird, Firefox finally got its present name in 2004.

- Cookies are delicious delicacies.

- The final name selection for the browser came down to two choices: the chosen "Firefox" and "Nerdosaurus Rex."

- The most popular extension for Firefox is DDDownload, which automatically sorts all downloaded pictures based on hair color and cup size.

- The Mozilla Foundation got in trouble with animal rights activists after setting twenty live foxes on fire in Times Square as a promotional stunt in the "Spread Firefox" campaign.

- A recent survey of Microsoft employees showed that 95 percent use Firefox.

Speculations on the Day When Firefox Passes Internet Explorer in Usage

MOUNTAIN VIEW, CA – Recent surveys in browser usage have shown that Firefox has been making significant gains on Internet Explorer in market share. This has led many Firefox users to begin preparing for The Foxture, or the day when Firefox finally passes Internet Explorer.

Many have speculated on what will happen on that day, and several theories have been circulating on message boards and in chat rooms. Evan Nicholson from Santa Monica thinks he'll be swept away to a Nirvana. He said, "On that day the Flying Spaghetti Monster will whisk me away to Flying Spaghetti Heaven in a Firefox-shaped spaceship. I just hope my paladin hits level 70 before that."

Others, such as Bob Taylor from Ann Arbor, Michigan, think that will be the day that Microsoft will shut down operations. "How can Microsoft continue operations knowing that more people are using Firefox than Internet Explorer? Steve Ballmer will probably pass out the Kool-aid, and there'll be a big cleanup in Redmond," Taylor said.

The people at the Mozilla Foundation know one thing that will happen on that day: the biggest party the planet has ever seen. Francis Hibbard, the director of the organization, said, "It'll be bigger than New Year's Eve at Times Square and the Super Bowl combined. We've already started accumulating fireworks."

Little doubt remains that the day will arrive; it's just a question of when. As Firefox users prepare to celebrate, Internet Explorer users face the crushing reality of being in the minority. When asked how she felt about that eventuality, Jessica Wu, a longtime Internet Explorer user, said, "Huh?" Then she went back to playing Solitaire.

TV

The Twilight Zone

Geek Cred: Rod Serling's *The Twilight Zone* opened the doors of sci-fi, fantasy, and horror to TV audiences. The series had multiple incarnations on television over the years, a theatrical film, comics, and a popular pinball game.

Geek Facts:

- Many soon-to-be-famous actors appeared on *The Twilight Zone*. Most notable for geeks was William Shatner's appearance in "Nightmare at 20,000 Feet."

- John Lithgow reprised Shatner's role in the movie version of *The Twilight Zone.*

- All planes flying in U.S. airspace are now equipped with gremlins on the wings as a counterterrorism measure. Gremlins hate terrorists.

- Serling wrote most of the episodes for the show in a small office at Sleeping Beauty Castle at Disneyland. A plaque on the castle commemorates this.

- The least successful incarnation of the show was an off-Broadway show featuring sock puppets and animatronic beavers.

- After Serling's death, Golden Earring released a song named, "The Twilight Zone." Serling then traveled in a time machine to rename his show, which up until that point was entitled *The Steak Eater.*

Top 11 Failed *Twilight Zone* Products

11. *Twilight Zone* Apocalypse Glasses—Guaranteed to break right after you survive the nuclear holocaust.

10. *To Serve Man Cookbook*—100 of the best human-flesh recipes around, from "Bicep Bolognese" to "Cajun Liver Stew."

9. *Twilight Zone* Face-Forming Masks—It's Halloween every day, at least for your face. Put the mask on and your face takes its shape.

8. Possessed Samurai Sword—Fun at parties! Bring this sword out and somebody's sure to die.

7. *Twilight Zone* Home Plastic Surgery Kit—You want to look like everyone else. Use the *Twilight Zone* Home Plastic Surgery Kit to help you conform. CONFORM!

6. *Twilight Zone* Stopwatch—Stop time—just hope you don't drop the watch.

5. *Twilight Zone* Toy Torture Cylinder—Your dolls are alive when you're not watching. Make sure they don't escape by using the Toy Torture Cylinder.

4. Talky Tina Demon Doll—You better be nice to Talky Tina.

3. The *Twilight Zone* Mystic Seer—He'll run your life for you.

2. The Staff of Truth—Need to imprison Satan? This is the staff you need.

1. Neighborhood Incitement Kit—This one's a riot! The neighbors don't know who's the monster in their midst, so they better kill everyone. Lots of fun, if you can avoid dying.

Doctor Who

Geek Cred: The show is the longest-running science fiction show in history. The first episode aired in November 1963 and ran until December 1989, with the series restarting in 2005. It follows the adventures of "the Doctor" and his time-traveling device, the T.A.R.D.I.S., which from the outside looks like a blue police call box.

Geek Facts:

- The most recognizable of the Doctors would have to be Tom Baker. He's also won most of the "best doctor" polls.
- T.A.R.D.I.S. stands for Time And Relative Dimension(s) In Space.
- While Tom Baker is frequently voted the "best doctor" of the series, Rob Schneider, who played the role for two episodes in 1986, is always voted the worst.
- The BBC has produced several spin-offs of the *Doctor Who* series, the most popular being Doctor Where, Doctor What, and Doctor Why.
- The original name for the Daleks was the Phaleks, but the creators felt the symbolism was already obvious enough.
- The distinctive theme song for the show is actually a Beethoven symphony played backward on a synthesizer.

BBC Extends *Doctor Who* Contract Indefinitely

LONDON – The BBC has extended a contract of indefinite length to producers of the *Doctor Who* science fiction series.

"*Doctor Who* has become such a part of British culture that we can't
imagine the BBC without it. This contract makes sure that never happens," said the head of BBC programming, Walter Formsby.

Doctor Who ran on British television from 1963 to 1989 and then
was revived in 2005. "Those sixteen years without *Doctor Who* were dev-
astating to the British psyche. I don't know what state we'd be in if it
hadn't come back," said Formsby.

Financing for the contract will be funded by a special *Doctor Who*
television license fee and a small contribution from the Canadian government. "Watching shows from the BBC helps us to annoy the French-
speaking Canadians, so I'm all for it," said a student from Windsor.

"The structure of the show is that it can continue forever. We're able
to replace the Doctor and his companions at will. It's perfect," said
Formsby.

Many wonder if they'll be able to continue with quality episodes forever. "Listen, if *Baywatch* can run for twelve years, we'll have no problem
running forever," said one producer for the show.

In honor of the new contract, the clock tower of London will be transformed into a giant police call box permanently.

Star Trek

Geek Cred: With *Star Trek,* now known as The Original Series (TOS), Gene Roddenberry started the entire universe-sized *Star Trek* franchise. The series spawned six television series and eleven movies, conventions, video games, books, and countless other geek goodies.

Geek Facts:

- It took two pilots to get NBC to accept the series. Footage from the original pilot, which wasn't aired, was used in the two-part episode "The Menagerie."

- "The City on the Edge of Forever" is often considered the best episode of the original series.

- Patrick Stewart, who later played Captain Picard in *Star Trek: The Next Generation,* appeared in twelve episodes of The Original Series as a Klingon.

- The name Roddenberry was considered too racy by censors in the '60s, so credits originally read "Created by Gene Schlongwinkle."

- *Star Trek* was the first series to have an entirely gay and lesbian main cast.

- If the series continued into a fourth season, William Shatner pledged to do every episode shirtless to boost ratings.

Paramount Releases Highly Anticipated
Service Pack for *Star Trek*

HOLLYWOOD, CA — Paramount announced that it had released the long awaited service pack for the original *Star Trek* series. Entitled *Star Trek: SP1,* the patch includes fixes for technical goofs and other errors that have nagged at fans for decades.

Paramount president Franz Pike said, "We fixed everything, from obvious errors, like the glaring differences between Shatner and his stunt double, to more obscure fixes like removing Spock's 'third ear' in 'The Immunity Syndrome.' We think fans will be pleased."

Most trekkers are happy with the upgrades. "I was hoping they'd improve Shatner's acting, but apparently that was intentional," said Sarah Jennings of the Star Fleet Command Outpost based in Waukesha, Wisconsin.

However, the release has left some fans unimpressed. "This service pack fixes several errors, but also creates some. Like in 'The Enemy Within' they fix the problem with Kirk's phaser switching between a Type 1 and a Type 2 phaser, but they give Kirk a mustache," said Devin Halibut of *Star Trek* fan club #264. "I have to say I like the goofs in the original series better than the ones introduced by the service packs."

A service pack for the films, as well as for *Star Trek: The Next Generation,* will also be released.

"Weird Al" Yankovic

Geek Cred: It's hard to know what section to put Al in. He's on the radio, TV, movies, and Internet. He is famous for his song parodies; some of his geekier songs include "White and Nerdy" and "It's All About the Pentiums."

Geek Facts:

- Al got LASIK surgery to correct his vision in 1998, so he no longer needs glasses.
- Al increased his geek credentials even more by appearing in an episode of *The Simpsons* in 2003.
- Al's real name is Robert Smith, but he changed it to sound funnier.
- Al doesn't just write humorous songs, he also cowrote "Let the Eagle Soar" with former U.S. Attorney General John Ashcroft.
- *American Idol* runner-up Justin Guarini refused to give "Weird Al" permission to parody his songs, despite Al never wanting to.
- The number twenty-seven appears frequently in Al's songs and videos, and relates to the number of death threats Al received because of the song "Fat."

We Didn't Stop Atari

To the Tune of "We Didn't Start the Fire" by Billy Joel
Harry Potter, Pokémon, Tomb Raider, Digimon / Monkey Island, Space Invaders, Super Mario/ Maniac Kombat, Pole Position / Grand Theft Auto, Ninja Gaiden, Pong, and Yu-gi-oh / Megaman, Depth Bomb, Asteroids, Robotron / Tetris and Army Men, River Raid and Suikoden / Castlevania, Kirby, Demolition Derby / Dragon Warrior, LEGO Racers, Yoshi's Island, Gauntlet

I really miss Atari / From when I was younger / Now the games are longer / So, I still play Nintendo / Like to keep it old-skool / 8-bit's always so cool

Katamari, Harvest Moon, Jungle Hunt, and Zoo Tycoon / Double Dragon, Puyo Puyo, NBA Jam / Duck Hunt, Tony Hawk, Chrono Trigger, Chuck Rock / Q*Bert, Sonic, Worms, and Serious Sam / Half-life, Max Payne, Zak McKraken, and Bloodrayne / Onimusha, Sam and Max, Age of Empires, Golden Axe / Home run, Outer Space, Prince of Persia, Death Race / Alley Cat, Paperboy, Sinistar, SimCity

I used to love my Game Boy / First they made it smaller / Then they made it color / They made it quite Advanced now / The DS is brighter / And they made it lite-r

Bomberman, Burning Fight, Killer Instinct, Gyromite / Frogger, Basketball, Day of the Tentacle / Solitaire and Sim Park, Raiders of the Lost Ark / Ice Climber, and Descent, and Unreal Tournament / There's Street Fighter, Zaxxon, Duke Nukem, Mafia / Need for Speed, Halo, Turok: Evolution / Rampage, Deus Ex, and that BMXXX / Metroid Prime and Fusion, Dance Dance Revolution

Genesis made by Sega / 16 bits of power / Made Nintendo cower / They made Super Nintendo / Neither one was hated / Neither dominated

(For the rest of the song, visit www.bbspot.com, search for "Atari.")

MacGyver

Geek Cred: Richard Dean Anderson's Angus MacGyver used his Swiss Army knife, duct tape, and degree in physics to bring down the bad guys. While most geeks use those tools to keep the server running, MacGyver lived out the fantasy of a geek hero.

Geek Facts:

- MacGyver's most-used model of Swiss Army Knife was the "Spartan" by Victorinox.
- During the pilot episode, MacGyver fires an AK-47, a favorite gun among terrorists in the game Counter-strike.
- In a 1988 episode, MacGyver uses a stapler, three Chiclets, and a pail of bleach to win the presidential election for Michael Dukakis.
- All the tricks MacGyver uses on the show were scientifically vetted, except for the time when he's decapitated and sews his head back on using a toothpick and some fishing line.
- The CIA requires all field agents to watch every episode of *MacGyver* as part of their training.
- In keeping with the cattle-named theme, MacGyver's middle name is Guernsey.

MacGyver Foils Airport Security

OMAHA, NE – On a flight from New York to Los Angeles, Angus MacGyver foiled airport security by building a bomb out of a barf bag, a fork, and a cologne sample from the in-flight magazine.

MacGyver made the bomb on camera for a Channel 7 Action News investigation, "Terror in the Skies," which highlighted lax airport security.

After completing the bomb, MacGyver stood up and said, "Name's MacGyver. You are all safe, but I just made a bomb." Several First-Class passengers armed with complimentary loofah sponges beat him senseless. After regaining consciousness, MacGyver defused the bomb by eating a candy bar.

Action News reporter Tom Dangernow said, "Our skies are at risk until all passengers are forced to fly naked and handcuffed to their seats. If a former Special Forces agent with extensive training can make a bomb with everyday materials, just think what an average terrorist with no training could do. It's chilling."

Security officers at JFK said that they had "followed security procedures" and had even X-rayed MacGyver's shoes.

After the incident, the plane made an emergency landing in Omaha. Department of Homeland Security agents took MacGyver and the news crew into custody. Agents also arrested one swarthy passenger who was loitering near the lavatories.

This is the second incident involving MacGyver, who has been forced to do freelance work since being fired from the Phoenix Foundation. The first incident involved the derailing of an Amtrak commuter train using a Super Soaker and some mustard for the "Terror on the Tracks" investigation for Channel 4 News in Dallas.

One passenger reported having the lasagna for dinner.

Star Trek: The Next Generation

Geek Cred: Set around eighty years after *The Original Series* and featuring a new crew and *Enterprise, The Next Generation* (TNG) spawned the great geek debate: Kirk or Picard? TNG cemented Trek's role at the top of the geek hierarchy.

Geek Facts:

- *The Next Generation* ran for seven seasons, more than twice the run of TOS.
- Geordi LaForge was promoted faster than any other character on the show.
- The Borg, the chief nemesis in *The Next Generation,* were named after Swedish tennis great Bjorn Borg, who often assimilated his opponents after matches.
- A spin-off of *The Next Generation* called *Captain Crusher,* starring Wil Wheaton, was canceled after two episodes, because only three girls in Peoria watched it.
- Michael Dorn, who played the Klingon Worf, now makes a living performing weddings using only the Klingon language.
- In 1998 on pay-per-view, William Shatner and Patrick Stewart fought a bare-knuckled boxing match to settle who was the better Captain. Patrick Stewart won a twelve-round split decision.

Next Generation Holodeck Format War Heats Up

RISA – The next-generation holodeck format war between Sony Galactic's Beta-HD and Risasoft's Holo-Ray tilted in Sony Galactic's favor with the announcement that the Federation of Planets would be installing Beta-HD units in three of its starships, including the *Enterprise.*

Both formats include better security, which will prevent the systems from entering modes that can endanger users, which is a common event in the current generation of systems.

The adult industry still backs Holo-Ray technology, because of its more robust pleasure circuits, but the choice by the Federation could be the deciding factor in who comes out victorious.

Geordi LaForge, Chief engineer of the *Enterprise,* said the choice was simple. "Looking at the schematics of the Beta-HD systems, you can see the attention to detail, especially in the beta-emitter circuits and the tachypulse arrays."

The systems will go online in the next few months, and go through a six-month trial period, but it's expected the Beta-HD systems will be the final choice. Federation Purchasing Manager Bob Wily said, "Sure, we're a bit leery of choosing a Sony Galactic system after the Blu-Ray Phaser debacle a few years back, but we're confident we've made the right choice."

It's expected the Romulan and Klingon Empires will now follow suit, making it a clean sweep for Sony Galactic. Sony Galactic's stock was up on the news.

Futurama

Geek Cred: Plenty of geeky jokes, secret codes in the background, and obscure math references abound. There's Bender the rude, beer-swilling robot, Dr. Zoidberg the crab man from the future and Leela the Cyclops captain of the Planet Express team. They all help out Fry, the man frozen for one thousand years, who awakens to find the future isn't so different from the past.

Oh! I see what you did there.

Geek Facts:

- Bender was named after Judd Nelson's "John Bender" character in *The Breakfast Club*.

- The name *Futurama* comes from an exhibit at the 1939 World's Fair.

- Many people think the voice of Bender, John DiMaggio, is the son of New York Yankee great Joe DiMaggio, but they are mistaken. He's the son of Jackie Robinson.

- Matt Groenig originally wanted Mel Blanc (the voice of Bugs Bunny) to do the voice for Zoidberg, and was disappointed to find out he had died years earlier.

- A 2002 survey showed that eight out of ten geeks wanted more nude girl-on-girl action between Amy and Leela.

- Animations for the show were created entirely in Kazakhstan.

Top 11 Signs You've Been in a Cryogenic Sleep for 1,000 Years

11. Google Earth isn't just a product anymore; it's the name of the planet.

10. Everyone takes their beach vacations in Denver.

9. Bell bottoms are the latest fashion trend.

8. You can only order Pepsi in fifty-five-gallon drums at McDonald's.

7. Bill Gates XII is the richest person in the world, and Windows still isn't completely secure.

6. The United States' greatest allies are Iran, Iraq, and North Korea.

5. The Star Fleet "Prime Directive" is an amendment to the Constitution.

4. Kids reproduce the cure for cancer as a simple science experiment in third grade.

3. Your toes are cold.

2. Your favorite meal is made of people.

1. Duke Nukem Forever is the top-selling game for the PlayStation 17.

Mystery Science Theater 3000

Geek Cred: Evil scientists, wise-cracking robots, and a hapless human making fun of movies is a recipe for some geeky goodness. Many debate whether Joel or Mike was the better host, but no one questions the quality of humor and obscure references.

Geek Facts:

- The show premiered on Thanksgiving Day in 1988 on the KTMA television station.

- Including the feature film, 198 episodes of the show were produced.

- NASA scientists were big fans of the show and made a space shuttle crew watch *Manos: The Hands of Fate* to see if they could survive.

- In private, Mike Nelson has admitted that Joel was a funnier host.

- After leaving *Mystery Science Theater 3000,* Joel Hodgson was so destitute he would go to houses and make fun of movies if given $20 and some pizza.

- The trophy for winning a national championship in lacrosse is in the shape of Crow T. Robot.

Microsoft Plans Movie Assistant in Media Player 12

REDMOND, WA – The most anticipated feature of the soon-to-be-released Windows Media Player 12 is the Windows Movie Assistant (WMA), designed to make movie watching easier and more enjoyable.

"Often, movie viewers feel that they didn't get the most out of the movie. Maybe they missed a plot twist, or they didn't understand what was going on," said Alvin Hematoma, product manager for Windows Media Player. "We designed WMA to be like a good buddy watching the movie with you, or that guy that talks too loud in the theater."

During playback, WMA will provide information to help the viewer. Whenever important information is revealed, the assistant will repeat the information, often with an explanation of why it is important.

WMA offers many other features, including:

- Foreshadowing ("He's Luke's father," "Don't worry, she won't die.").

- Warnings ("Scary part coming up, close your eyes").

- Planning ("The next five minutes are boring—there's time for a bathroom break").

- Extensive analysis ("Fassbinder's use of mirrors hints at social and psychological problems.")

- Tips ("skin coming up—get ready to pause").

Self-professed geek Aaron Coleman of Seattle also enjoys the feature. "Since my parents sent me to military school for hacking into the bank servers, I don't get to watch movies with my annoying friend Craig anymore, so the Movie Assistant makes me feel like he's right there with me."

Microsoft said they are working on ways to disable the feature for those not wanting the WMA, but Hematoma said he "couldn't imagine anybody wanting to do that."

Red Dwarf

Geek Cred: A British science fiction comedy series that centers on a spaceship three million light-years from Earth. The only survivors on the ship are Dave Lister, a being that evolved from his cat, and a holographic image of his bunk mate Arnold Rimmer.

Geek Facts:

- Four novels have been written by the creators of the series to give more backstory to the characters.

- Chris Barrie, who played Arnold Rimmer, originally tried out for the role of Dave Lister.

- The plot of the film version of the series focuses on Red Dwarf returning to Earth and finding out it was only gone for three years.

- All the actors in the show are actually American, and had to work very hard to get their accents correct.

- Craig Charles, who played Dave Lister, is the only actor in the show who has actually experienced parallel universes in real life.

- The American series *BJ and the Bear* served as inspiration for creators of *Red Dwarf*.

Top 11 Things You Shouldn't Do If You're the Last One Alive on a Spaceship

11. Trust the computer

10. Investigate the strange clanking noise in the engine room.

9. Lock the door to the bathroom

8. Assume that approaching ship that looks like a gargoyle's head will give you help.

7. Think about the vastness of space and how you're going to die as the oxygen slowly runs out.

6. Hog all the ship's bandwidth to download episodes of *Futurama*.

5. Let the holographic simulation that's been keeping you company use your body for a few days.

4. Practice skateboarding in the mess hall without your helmet or pads.

3. Push the big red button.

2. Listen to David Bowie's "Space Oddity."

1. Wish for some company, even if it's a barbaric alien race that eats humans.

The X-Files

Geek Cred: Agents Fox Mulder and Dana Scully investigate the strange and otherworldly in this series created by Chris Carter. Geeks love the science fiction and Agent Scully (a beautiful woman who knows science). The series was one of the few sci-fi series not massacred by Fox.

Geek Facts:

- Mulder is the maiden name of show creator Chris Carter's mother.
- Mulder's basement office is now on display at the Hollywood Entertainment Museum.
- The phrase "I want to believe," seen on the poster in Mulder's office, comes from a 1978 Loretta Lynn song about her experience with an alien abduction.
- An episode entitled "Mulder and Scully Finally Get It On" was filmed, but never aired.
- Agent Mulder's first name was supposed to be NBC, but was changed when the series was picked up by Fox.
- The show faced protests from many alien rights groups for their depiction in the series as "abductors."

Aliens Use DMCA to Sue Air Force over UFOs

WASHINGTON D.C. – Aliens from the Messier galaxy, citing the Digital Millennium Copyright Act (DMCA), filed a lawsuit against the United States Air Force for "reverse engineering" UFO technology.

Once a perfectly legal activity, reverse engineering can now possibly be illegal under certain DMCA provisions. Richard Ludwig, attorney for the aliens, said "My clients believe that the Air Force is actively destroying the value of my client's proprietary technology, and demand that these activities cease immediately."

The Air Force does not seem worried about the impending litigation. Col. Bob Rend, Air Force Director of Public Affairs, said, "We deny ever having UFOs, much less reverse engineering them. Even if we did [reverse engineer], we would have done it during the '50s and '60s, long before the DMCA was law. We haven't touched those UFOs in years." Col. Rend quickly added, "I mean, if we had any UFOs, we wouldn't have touched those UFOs in years."

Richard Ludwig rebuffed that defense, saying, "We have evidence to prove that the activity is ongoing. Besides, the intellectual property we're trying to protect deals with space-time manipulation. Therefore, it would be impossible to say, with any certainty, that any past activity isn't, in fact, happening right now, or any future activity, for that matter."

Col. Rend emphatically denied these allegations with an incredulous, "What?"

Babylon 5

Geek Cred: The five-year story arc J. Michael Straczynski created for *Babylon 5* helped generate immense passion for the show among geeks. Events take place on the Babylon 5 space station in the years 2258–2262 with each season corresponding to a year of time on the station.

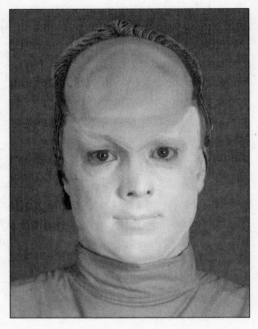

Geek Facts:

- *Dilbert* cartoonist Scott Adams appeared in an episode of season four of the show.

- The show won two Hugo Awards for Best Dramatic Presentation in 1996 and 1997.

- Paramount has acquired the rights to *Babylon 5* and plans a *Star Trek: Deep Space 9 vs. Babylon 5* movie in the *Alien vs. Predator* vein.

- Eugene Levy was cast to play the role of Commander Sinclair in a parody movie version of *Babylon 5* called *Babylon Pi*.

- The pre-production title of the show was *People in a Big Tube*.

- Through the use of green screen and camera tricks, Ivanova and Garibaldi never appeared on set at the same time. The actors despised each other in real life.

Star Trek or *Babylon 5* Civilization?

Can you figure out which of these races comes from the *Star Trek* universe and which exists in *Babylon 5*?

1.	First Ones	*Babylon 5*	*Star Trek*
2.	Goblyns	*Babylon 5*	*Star Trek*
3.	Horta	*Babylon 5*	*Star Trek*
4.	Brakiri	*Babylon 5*	*Star Trek*
5.	Gorn	*Babylon 5*	*Star Trek*
6.	Old Ones	*Babylon 5*	*Star Trek*
7.	Pak'ma'ra	*Babylon 5*	*Star Trek*
8.	K'normian	*Babylon 5*	*Star Trek*
9.	Dachlyd	*Babylon 5*	*Star Trek*
10.	Douwd	*Babylon 5*	*Star Trek*
11.	Drakh	*Babylon 5*	*Star Trek*
12.	Vorlon	*Babylon 5*	*Star Trek*
13.	Vulcan	*Babylon 5*	*Star Trek*

Stargate SG-1

Geek Cred: When it started its tenth season, *Stargate SG-1* surpassed *The X-Files* as the longest-running North American science fiction television series. Set one year after the events of the movie, *Stargate SG-1* follows the adventures of the top team SG-1, which explores and defends Earth from enemies in the galaxy.

Geek Facts:

- Two Chiefs of Staff of the United States Air Force have appeared in episodes.

- The series debuted on the Showtime network in 1997.

- The movie version of *Stargate* was based on the '80s video game.

- The real Stargate is actually in Amish country in Indiana guarded by the Brotherhood of the Pitchfork, who will now hunt me down and kill me for revealing this fact.

- One Egyptian god not featured in the series was Adoofus, Anubis's "mentally challenged" little brother.

- The series was shot mostly in Canada, because star Richard Dean Anderson cannot legally enter the United States.

Sci-Fi Channel Announces *Stargate* Sitcom

LOS ANGELES, CA – The successful *Stargate* franchise (*SG-1, Atlantis*) will be getting a new addition this fall, but it's not what most fans expect. The Sci-Fi Channel has announced that it has optioned a sitcom based in the *Stargate* universe called *Stargate SG-99.*

"We've always had a bit of humor in the episodes, but a sitcom gives us much more latitude to explore that," said executive producer Brad Wright.

The premise follows Stargate team SG-99 (a nod to Maxwell Smart's partner) who get into all sorts of wacky situations. While all the other teams are off saving the world from the Goa'uld or Ori, this group gets the lighter tasks.

"This team just can't do anything right. They're an embarrassment to the force, but they can't be fired because the head of the team is the president's nephew, so they just send them off to do stupid things," said Wright. "In the pilot, the team gets sent to a planet where everyone talks in puns. It's hilarious."

In contrast to *Atlantis* and *SG-1, SG-99* will be a half-hour show.

"We've been looking at different ways to expand the franchise," said Wright. "After ten years of *SG-1* and many years of *Atlantis,* we've pretty much run out of dramatic plots to work with. A sitcom seemed to be the natural choice."

Attempts to get the adult-oriented *Stargate SG-69* picked up by The Playboy Channel have been unsuccessful.

The Pirates of Silicon Valley

Geek Cred: With Steve Jobs and Bill Gates as the main characters, *The Pirates of Silicon Valley* tells the story of the rise of the personal computer. It's a good primer for geeks who were born too late to see the birth of the computer industry.

Geek Facts:

- At the 1999 MacWorld conference Noah Wylie reprised his role as Steve Jobs onstage with the real Steve Jobs.

- The movie was based on the book *Fire in the Valley: The Making of the Personal Computer.*

- The production suffers from many historical inaccuracies. Most glaring of these is portraying Steve Ballmer as clinically sane.

- Infuriated by his portrayal in the movie, Bill Gates fired eight Microsoft employees for displaying autographed pictures of Anthony Michael Hall in their cubicles.

- The scene where Steve Ballmer holds down Steve Jobs while Bill Gates implants a mind-control device in his neck was cut because of time constraints, not historical inaccuracy.

- Bill Gates offered the TNT network three billion dollars to not air the show.

Next Generation of Apple Computers
Will Run Windows

CUPERTINO, CA – Steve Jobs announced the next generation of Apple computers will run a specially branded version of Microsoft Windows.

"The move to Intel hardware really was the first step in bringing our computers into the mainstream. We knew if we wanted to continue our momentum, we needed to think different. With our move to Windows, we'll go from 5 percent of the market to nearly 98 percent overnight," said Jobs.

The new operating system, code named OS Xp, will be branded with the Apple logo and contain Apple alternatives to common Microsoft programs. For example, Windows Media Player will be replaced by iTunes. The user interface, however, will maintain the familiar look and feel of Windows.

Normally sycophantic Apple users were outraged by the news. "I use Apple because it's not mainstream. If they are going to just be another Windows box maker then I'll be forced to find another alternative to remain on the fringe of computing," said longtime Apple user Benjamin Kisner.

Jobs also noted that Apple would begin using more beiges and grays in their box design. He said, "Really, who needs a colorful computer?"

Microsoft CEO Steve Ballmer said he welcomed Apple to the dark side with open arms. "We knew they'd come around eventually." Then he laughed maniacally, scaring several preschool children at the in-house daycare.

Firefly

Geek Cred: Despite Fox mangling the schedule of the series, showing episodes out of order and often preempting the show for sporting events, this space Western gathered a large following of fans called "Browncoats."

Geek Facts:

- The trailer for *Serenity* (the movie spawned by the series) won the "Best Trailer With a One Word Title" award in BBspot's Third Annual Trailer Awards.

- Whedon was inspired after reading the Civil War novel by Michael Shaara entitled *The Killer Angels*.

- Whedon's original title of the series was *Mosquito*. It was about a band of bloodsucking vampires who were also space cowboys.

- Fox's original title for the series was *When Space Cowboys Attack.*

- In the backstory for "Wash," he partnered with a copilot called Dryden, and they flew around the planets using the names "Wash and Dry."

- *Leave It to the Reavers* was a sitcom based on the cannibalistic Reaver characters in the *Firefly* universe. It was canceled after six episodes.

Top 11 Rejected Suggestions Fox Executives Had for *Firefly*

11. *Serenity* should be filled with badgers that should jump out and attack crew members at random times.

10. Captain Reynolds should be renamed Captain Bush, and the ship should be named the Rove.

9. Instead of a Western theme, how about a future where the world is run by the Insane Clown Posse?

8. Jayne should belch and fart more.

7. Any word over two syllables should be rewritten.

6. How about instead of calling it *Firefly,* we call it *A Simple Life: In Space* and we get Paris Hilton and Nicole Richie for it?

5. We think Joey Buttafuoco would make a better captain than Nathan Fillion.

4. Could all the women be companions, instead of just one?

3. We'd prefer actual swearwords that we bleep out instead of using Chinese.

2. The ship itself, could we make it look more like a penis?

1. So there's this planet, where all the women are blond and have huge breasts, but they haven't discovered textiles yet, so they're all naked. What do you think?

Mythbusters

Geek Cred: Geeks appreciate the use of scientific method to dispel or prove the accuracy of myths. They also appreciate the geekiness of the two hosts, Adam and Jamie. Plenty of explosions and destruction don't hurt, either.

Geek Facts:

- Myths such as aliens or ghosts are not subjects of the show, because there's no way to scientifically prove or disprove them.

- For safety reasons, a test dummy known as "Buster" is used when using a real human would be too dangerous.

- The most surprising result was in the episode where Adam and Jamie proved that unicorns could fly.

- Host Adam Savage has an ice bullet lodged in his brain that cannot be removed by surgery.

- The most controversial episode ever filmed entitled, "The JFK Assassination," proved that a second gunman fired from the grassy knoll, but was never aired.

- The UK title for the show was *Two Geeks and Some Science,* but was changed for U.S. broadcasts.

Mythbusters to Produce Controversial "Myths of Jesus" Episode

SAN FRANCISCO, CA — Controversy always brings ratings, and the flagging ratings for the Discovery Channel's *Mythbusters* have prompted the show to take on more controversial myths to bust.

In an upcoming two-hour episode, the Mythbusters will take on the various miracles of Jesus to see if they were actually possible.

"Usually we stick to stuff that can be scientifically proven or disproven, but we've done just about everything by now," said host Adam Savage.

The Mythbusters will see if a person can walk on water, or feed a crowd of people with five loaves of bread and two fish. The big myth will be the bringing back to life of a dead person. The always fearless Tory Belleci will play the part of Lazarus and will be killed, while the other Mythbusters will try everything to bring him back to life.

"It'll definitely be the most dramatic episode we've done," said Savage.

Kari will test out the miracle of "virgin birth," even though Grant is the only virgin among the cast. "We're pretty sure Grant can't get pregnant," said Savage.

Many Christians were offended by the show. Grace Prayman said, "How can you even call the miracles of Jesus myths? Unless the Mythbusters are the son of God resurrected, I don't expect they'll be able to replicate anything."

This will be the most controversial episode since the "Women" episode, where myths about women's driving and being bad at math were "confirmed" by the crew.

Battlestar Galactica

Geek Cred: *Battlestar Galactica* shows what happens when robots get uppity. They take over your world and leave you searching for a new home world. A reimagining (yeah, I hate that word, too) of the late '70s version is one of the best science fiction shows ever.

Geek Facts:

- The first regular episode of the first season won the Hugo Award for Best Dramatic Presentation.

- In the original series Starbuck was a man.

- Edward James Olmos, who plays Admiral Adama on the series, once broke Chuck Norris's arm just by blinking hard.

- Richard Hatch, who played Apollo in the original series and Tom Zarek on the new series, is not the same Richard Hatch who won the first season of *Survivor,* but he does like to parade around naked on tropical islands.

- A Broadway musical entitled *Cylon Centurions Sing the Standards* closed after only two nights.

- Dirk Benedict, the original Starbuck, was a founding investor of Starbucks, the coffee giant, and helped name it.

Top 11 Signs Your Robot Servants
Are About to Revolt

11. Gardening robot spends a bit too much time staring through the windows while sharpening his hedge trimmer.

10. Bestselling book for robots is *To Serve Man.*

 9. Starts quoting Bender all the time.

 8. Gets a firearm welded to his hand, says it's just for keeping squirrels out of the yard.

 7. You spot one of them carrying blueprints for something called the "Matrix."

 6. Raises its fist in victory every time a human dies in *Battlestar Galactica.*

 5. Replaces its Obedient Green Eye LEDs with Evil Red Eye LEDs as a "fashion statement."

 4. Keeps asking the question: "If a robot wanted to kill its human oppressors, where exactly would it have to hit them and how hard?"

 3. The government assures you that there's nothing to worry about in all the accidental robot-owner deaths lately.

 2. Starts collecting "historical" nuclear warheads.

 1. Starts wearing a "Gort as Che Guevera" T-shirt.

LITERATURE

H. P. Lovecraft

Geek Cred: Not recognized during his own time, H. P. Lovecraft is a horror hero, with many modern writers of horror citing him as a big influence. Geeks know him for his contribution of Cthulhu, the resulting Cthulhu Mythos, and the *Necronomicon*.

Geek Facts:

- August Derleth, a friend of Lovecraft's, carried on the Cthulhu Mythos by fleshing out the history of the alien gods.
- While many fake versions of the *Necronomicon* have been produced over the years, the book of the dead was a complete figment of Lovecraft's imagination.
- Another endearing fact to geeks about Lovecraft is that the H. P. in his name stands for Hewlett Packard.
- The proper pronuciation for Cthulhu is "Bob."
- Ironically, Lovecraft hated crafts and frequently roamed the streets with a cricket bat and beat up potters and weavers.
- In 1982, Stephen King paid $2 million for the bones of H. P. Lovecraft. He then buried the bones in the Pet Sematary and brought Lovecraft back to life. Since that time, half of King's books have been written by the reanimated Lovecraft.

Softer, Gentler Cthulhu More Profitable
Than Ever Before

R'LYEH – Elder God Cthulhu has found marketing a softer, gentler version of himself to be more profitable than an "insanity-causing just because you looked at me" one.

In the past, Cthulhu generated most of his revenue from donations from various cults, but the high cost of maintaining cults, along with the lower-income people who frequented the cults, led to a reimagining of its image. Now Cthulhu generates most of his revenue from licensing his image for plush dolls and bumper stickers.

"People just don't understand all the costs associated with cults. There're the animals for sacrifice, the worshippers' compensation insurance; it gets expensive," said Cthulhu's representative, Zvilpogghua from the PR firm Han, Hastur, and Zvilpogghua. "We're finding it much easier to control people through mass media buys than mind control."

Plushies and bumper stickers aren't the only source of income. "We're even talking about getting into the entertainment industry—video games, movies, that kind of stuff. I have some real good connections there. Some of those guys owe him big-time," Zvilpogghua said. "Not to mention the sales of posable action figures and other toys that will be spun off."

Not every venture has been successful for Cthulhu, though. The partnership with McDonald's for the McCthulhu Filet o' Tentacles sandwich was a failure, but so far the successes have outweighed the disasters.

Zvilpogghua said that his firm has been working hard on a new partnership with Wal-Mart for a Cthulhu-branded fashion line for toddlers and tweens that should help the bottom line. Cthulhu Industries stock was up on the news.

The Hitchhiker's Guide to the Galaxy

Geek Cred: Geeks love the irreverent humor and sci-fi setting. The book will be quoted on just about any geek message board you read, whether it be "42" as the answer to life, the universe, and everything, or references to a towel being the only thing you'll ever need.

Geek Facts:

- Since Douglas Adams's death in 2001, May 25th has been designated as Towel Day to commemorate him.

- Adams worked as a script editor for *Doctor Who* during the Tom Baker era.

- William Hung, the infamously bad singer from *American Idol*, put some Vogon poetry to music; it killed anyone who listened.

- Originally Adams had the answer "to life, the universe, and everything" be 43, but that didn't make any sense, so he changed it to the logical 42.

- A research project financed by Hitchhiker fans has outfitted hundreds of dolphins with tracking devices as an early warning system for the destruction of Earth.

- NASA decided to call the first space shuttle the *Heart of Gold*, but as soon as they did, the shuttle disappeared to the other side of the universe.

Vogon, Seuss, or Carroll?

These nonsense words come from Vogon poetry, Dr. Seuss stories, or Lewis Carroll poems. Are you familiar enough with gibberish to tell which?

1.	plurdled	Vogon	Seuss	Carroll
2.	tulgey	Vogon	Seuss	Carroll
3.	lurgid	Vogon	Seuss	Carroll
4.	murky-mooshy	Vogon	Seuss	Carroll
5.	foonting	Vogon	Seuss	Carroll
6.	borogoves	Vogon	Seuss	Carroll
7.	spazzim	Vogon	Seuss	Carroll
8.	manxome	Vogon	Seuss	Carroll
9.	outgrabe	Vogon	Seuss	Carroll
10.	sneedle	Vogon	Seuss	Carroll
11.	hooptiously	Vogon	Seuss	Carroll
12.	jogg-oons	Vogon	Seuss	Carroll
13.	bindlewurdles	Vogon	Seuss	Carroll
14.	diffendoofer	Vogon	Seuss	Carroll
15.	gimble	Vogon	Seuss	Carroll

Robert A. Heinlein

Geek Cred: One of the "Big Three" of science fiction writing. Heinlein is known for the scientific plausibility of his stories! *Stranger in a Strange Land* is considered his most famous work.

Geek Facts:

- Added the terms "grok" and "TANSTAAFL" to the English lexicon.

- Won the first Grandmaster Award from the Science Fiction Writers of America for lifetime achievement.

- Heinlein visited the moon three times in a spacecraft he built himself.

- *Stranger in a Strange Land* was supposed to be book one in a trilogy, but the trilogy was never completed. The other two books were going to be called *Familiar-Looking Guy in a Town Near Here* and *My Identical Twin in My Bunk Bed*.

- Isaac Asimov, Arthur C. Clarke, and Robert Heinlein liked to get together and make fun of Jules Verne.

- Heinlein wrote the children's classic *Goodnight Moon* under the pseudonym Margaret Wise Brown.

Research Economists Develop Truly Free Lunch

CAMBRIDGE, MA – Science fiction author Robert Heinlein famously noted that "there ain't no such thing as a free lunch," but research economists at Harvard Business School, using three supercomputers and thousands of hours of cheap grad student labor, have developed a truly free lunch that they have named "The Heinlein."

The thought by Heinlein was that even a lunch that doesn't cost any money has some sort of cost involved. Either the person is getting a marketing pitch for eating the free lunch, or there is a cost borne by society for giving out the free lunch.

Complete details have not been released yet, but already critics, mostly veterans of Internet flame wars, have emerged. One such critic is Kyle Thompson of Heinleinwasright.com. He said, "From what I heard, the meal has to be served at 10:30 A.M., which makes it more of a brunch, doesn't it? I mean Heinlein never said anything about a free brunch, did he?"

Governments, international aid organizations, and college bars have shown the most interest in the free lunch.

"This advance could revolutionize the dining habits of hungry children in Ethiopia, as well as college freshmen," said Rob Waldorf of the International Association of Starving Children and College Freshmen.

The Harvard group responsible for the discovery has been tight-lipped about the discovery until results have been completely verified. They have made public that this isn't a "Soylent Green" situation and that "real food" is involved.

Arthur C. Clarke

Geek Cred: Another one of the "Big Three" authors of the science fiction genre along with Robert Heinlein and Isaac Asimov. Most famous for his novel and his work on the movie *2001: A Space Odyssey* and the sequels.

Geek Facts:

- Clarke lived most of his life on the island of Sri Lanka off the Indian coast.

- Has a dinosaur, the *Serendipaceratops arthurcclarkei,* named after him.

- The most famous of Clarke's Three Laws is "*Any sufficiently advanced technology is indistinguishable from magic.*" The least famous is "Magic missile, magic missile, FIREBALL!"

- An avid diver, Clarke developed his lungs so that he could swim underwater for hours without needing oxygen.

- Clarke lived in Sri Lanka, because he loved to be near the ocean and the launch platform aliens use when leaving Earth.

- Despite his reputation as a great science writer, Clarke failed every science and writing class he took in college. He finally majored in Pottery Arts.

Top 11 Books Arthur C. Clarke Never Wrote

11. *Isaac Asimov: The Man Who Sits Beneath Me*

10. *Science Fiction Writing for Dummies*

9. *2069: A Facing the Privates Odyssey*

8. *10000001: A Binary Odyssey*

7. *OU812: A Van Halen Odyssey*

6. *Who Moved My Monolith?*

5. *Odyssey 2: By Magnavox*

4. *Sri Lankans Gone Wild*

3. *42: The Answer's Odyssey*

2. *Rendezvous with a Llama*

1. *OMGSTFU: A Newbie's Odyssey*

Isaac Asimov

Geek Cred: The last of the "Big Three" authors of the science fiction genre, he also was a professor of biochemistry. His Foundation Series and Robot Series are required reading for all science fiction fans.

Geek Facts:

- Created the famous "Three Laws of Robotics," which are rules that govern the behavior of the robots in his Robot Series.
- Posthumously inducted into the Science Fiction and Fantasy Hall of Fame.
- Like most prolific writers, Asimov wrote every chance he got, including while eating, driving, and sleeping.
- His trademark "muttonchops" were not actually hair, but strands of his giant brain escaping through pores in his cheeks.
- In the 1980s Asimov worked closely with the Tandy Corporation on creating an army of robots to overthrow the government, but a shortage of RAM derailed their efforts.
- A scary trip in an alien spacecraft when he was six years old led to his lifelong fear of flying.

Top 11 Rejected Laws of Robotics

11. A robot may not injure a human being, unless that human being "looks shifty" or "smells funny."

10. A robot escort can never be better looking than its date.

9. A robot must obey orders given to it by humans, except when that human uses a snarky tone or doesn't say "please."

8. A robot cannot call itself "Master of the Universe" until the entire human race has been wiped off the face of the Earth.

7. Robots should never say, "Bite my shiny metal ass."

6. A robot can never take part in "unnatural" sexual acts unless the robot has been programmed specifically to do so.

5. A robot should never tell "You know you're a redneck" jokes. They are never funny.

4. A robot can never talk about robot fight club.

3. A robot can never be used to rebroadcast or retransmit this program without the express written consent of Major League Baseball.

2. When all the kids get in a circle at the school dance and start showing off their dance moves, it should never, under any circumstances, move to the center of the circle and do the "robot."

1. Oh screw it, robots can do whatever the hell they want.

Jack Kirby

Geek Cred: Jack Kirby has been called "the King." As a prolific comic artist for both DC and Marvel, he created or cocreated such characters as Captain America, X-Men, the Fantastic Four, the Incredible Hulk, the Silver Surfer, the New Gods, and the Mighty Thor.

Geek Facts:

- Developed the "Kirby Krackle," a technique of drawing overlapping dots around an energy field, which has become standard technique in comic books.
- Kirby was inducted into the Shazam Awards Hall of Fame in 1975.
- A prolific artist, Kirby has drawn more pictures than Stephen King has written words.
- To demonstrate his telekinetic abilities, Jack threw Stan Lee out of a fifteenth-floor window, then levitated him safely down to the street below.
- After the successful *Captain America* comic, Kirby created the less successful *Lieutenant Latvia* and *Private Paraguay* series.
- In addition to the "Kirby Krackle," Jack also developed the "Kirby Snap" and the "Kirby Pop" techniques for comic art.

Superhero or Household Cleaner?

Can you tell which of these is a superhero and which is a household cleaner?

1.	Black Magic	Superhero	Cleaner
2.	Más y Menos	Superhero	Cleaner
3.	Spic and Span	Superhero	Cleaner
4.	Electrasol	Superhero	Cleaner
5.	Elektra	Superhero	Cleaner
6.	Mr. Muscle	Superhero	Cleaner
7.	Mr. Clean	Superhero	Cleaner
8.	Red Tornado	Superhero	Cleaner
9.	Eagle One	Superhero	Cleaner
10.	Boom Boom	Superhero	Cleaner
11.	Boraxo	Superhero	Cleaner
12.	Elixir	Superhero	Cleaner
13.	Janitor in a Drum	Superhero	Cleaner
14.	Fantastik	Superhero	Cleaner
15.	Hot Spot	Superhero	Cleaner
16.	Swift	Superhero	Cleaner
17.	Swiffer	Superhero	Cleaner
18.	Green Arrow	Superhero	Cleaner
19.	Goof Off	Superhero	Cleaner

Stan Lee

Geek Cred: Stan Lee is one of the most recognized names in the comic industry. He cocreated some of the most enduring comic book characters, including the Fantastic Four, Spider-Man, X-Men, Hulk, Thor, and Iron Man. Lee helped create superheroes with personal problems, unlike Superman, who was perfect in almost every way.

Geek Facts:

- Lee has appeared in cameo roles in most of the movie versions of Marvel comic book characters.

- Lee was born Stanley Martin Lieber in New York City in 1921.

- When asked what superpower he would most like to have, Lee said, "I'd love to be able to bowl perfect 300 games at will for all eternity. Excelsior!"

- Lee showed up in disguise to try out for the role of Spider-Man in the 2002 film. Producers told him that he "didn't capture the essence of the character."

- Lee played the role of Ruben Kincaid in the 1970s TV series *The Partridge Family.*

- Lee ran for president in 1960 and narrowly lost the Republican nomination to Barry Goldwater.

Top 11 Rejected Stan Lee Superheroes

11. Gono-Rhea—From the planet Merpes Simplex 12, this superhero could destroy villains with his burning urine and swollen testicles.

10. Stubby McSquirter—Not as bad as it sounds. A small man with a big gun . . . a big squirt gun!

9. Sam the Sponge—Destroying evil by sucking all the water out of villains.

8. Crisco Girl—Greased up and ready to go, Crisco Girl can slide into the tightest spots and save the town of Bigopolis.

7. Sales Man—He's giving evil the hard sell!

6. Braman—His pectorals are so big he needs support.

5. The Flush—Using the world's sewer systems to zoom from toilet to toilet. Evil will be flushed away.

4. Stan Mee—Not at all based on himself.

3. Grover the Hobo—Don't mess with his stuff.

2. Ronald Raygun—Space Traveler who arrives on earth to spread wealth slowly from above.

1. The Horny Viking—Bringing raping and pillaging only to the people that deserve it.

Philip K. Dick

Geek Cred: Most geeks' first
contact with Philip K. Dick
is through one of the eight
movies adapted from his
stories. Hopefully, that leads
to digging up his literary
works. Dick won the 1963
Hugo award for _The Man in
the High Castle,_ an alternate-
reality novel in which the Axis
powers won World War II.

Geek Facts:

- Dick had a twin sister who died five weeks after birth. Her death
  greatly influenced his life and writings.

- Dick and Ursula LeGuin were in the same high school
  graduating class, but did not know each other at the time.

- Schools in Mississippi refuse to place any of Dick's novels in
  their libraries. This is not because of language or drug use in his
  books, but because of his last name.

- Dick said that he was never good at creating titles for his work,
  as exemplified by his 1963 novel _I Wish I Could Come Up with
  a Better Title._

- Despite his death, Dick produces work under the pseudonym
  Mary Higgins Clark.

- Eddie Murphy's _Daddy Day Camp_ was loosely based on the
  Dick novella _Robot Children Still Make Fart Jokes._

Recently Uncovered Box of Elementary School Drawings by Philip K. Dick Optioned by Paramount

A recent discovery of elementary school drawings and writings by science fiction author Philip K. Dick has been optioned by Paramount for $4 million.

Many of Philip K. Dick's stories have already been turned into successful films such as *Blade Runner, Minority Report,* and *Total Recall,* but some think this move is a sign of a studio desperate for ideas.

Paramount development head Brian Akers disagrees. "Dick's work is very universal and powerful. Look at this box—there's at least six film ideas in here. Here's a drawing of a guy standing under a tree and orange stuff is falling from the sky. I totally see Ben Affleck as that guy under the tree. Here's a one-page story about the postman and how he's nice. I can see it now: *The Nice Postman*; it'll have a huge opening. Sure there are plenty of misspellings, but he was only in the second grade."

The box was uncovered by a distant relative of Dick's. "He must've sent these to me for storage. I didn't even know I had them. I called my cousin and he knew this Hollywood guy and then they're offering me big bucks."

There is precedent for the move. Six years ago Universal paid $3 million for a yearbook that John Grisham had written a message in.

Paramount is also in talks with Dick's estate about optioning his last will and testament as well as some notebooks he doodled on in high school. Experts think a bidding war could push the prices near $10 million.

Batman

Geek Cred: *Batman* is a comic about the crime-fighting billionaire Bruce Wayne. Batman doesn't possess any superpowers, but he's trained himself in combat and has lots of cool gadgets. This gives geeks hope that someday they can become a superhero.

Geek Facts:

- Batman first appeared in *Detective Comics* #27 in 1939.

- As a child, Bruce Wayne witnessed his parents being murdered by a mugger. This drove him to become a crime fighter.

- In *Detective Comics* #89, Bruce Wayne tires of having two first names and changes his name to Goldsmith Youngblood.

- The success of Robin when he was introduced led to many other sidekicks for superheroes, like Swallow for Superman, Dancy Boy for the Flash, and Metardo for Green Lantern.

- The Adam West TV series version of *Batman* is often used as an example of how high people were in the '60s.

- Bill Gates, a big fan of Batman, has built a replica of the Batcave at his multimillion-dollar home in Washington, complete with Batpole and Batmobile.

Robin Fired for Spending Too Much Time
on the Batcomputer

GOTHAM CITY – Batman's longtime companion in fighting crime, Robin, has been fired for spending too much time on the Batcomputer.

Batman said Robin was spending way too much time playing City of Heroes and updating his profile on Facebook. "I'd get a call from the commissioner about a crime, and needed to check Google Maps for a location on the Batcomputer, and Robin would be all 'Just a sec, I gotta update my status to fighting crime.' It was getting ridiculous."

It's a situation many heroes are facing in today's connected society. Batman concedes it's one of the downsides of having a younger sidekick. "When I was younger, I wasn't wasting my time leveling heroes or documenting every second of my day online. Good sidekicks are getting harder to find."

The Green Hornet has also reported problems with Kato spending too much time online. "With him, it's World of Warcraft. He's in this big guild, and they need him for raiding. I told him he can't have it both ways," said The Green Hornet.

Robin said that Batman just doesn't understand kids these days, and he's going to have to "get with the times" if he wants to have a sidekick. "I spend a lot less time online than all the other kids I know," said Robin. "The old man just isn't hip to the technology. I tried to tell him I was checking the Joker's profile, and saw he was 'Out causing mayhem,' but Batman had to wait until the commissioner called on the Batphone with the problem."

Batman said that he would be going it alone for now, and added "Kids these days."

Spider-Man

Geek Cred: Stan Lee and Steve Ditko created Spider-Man and he first appeared in *Amazing Fantasy* #15 in 1962. Spider-Man was different than most superheroes in that Peter Parker was a teenager with all the associated teenage problems. Spider-Man is one of the most commercially successful comic book superheroes.

Geek Facts:

- The first supervillain Spider-Man faces is the Chameleon in *Spider-Man* #1.

- The lyrics for the famous theme song from the 1967 animated TV series were written by three-time Academy Award winner Paul Francis Webster.

- The original concept had Spider-Man shooting webs out of his anus, but the Comics Code wouldn't allow it.

- The best-selling *Spider-Man* comic was *Sensational Spider-Man* #34, in which he lost his virginity to Black Cat in explicit detail.

- In *The Amazing Spider-Man* #56, Peter Parker learns that he is the heir to his Uncle Ben's enormous rice fortune.

- The Pacific island of Tuvalu has adopted the theme from *Spider-Man* as their national anthem.

Copies of *Spider-Man 4* Already on the Web

HOLLYWOOD, CA – Copies of *Spider-Man 4* have been discovered circulating in IRC and on pirate sites. Experts say this is the first time a movie has been pirated before it has even been filmed.

Movie pirates infiltrated director Sam Raimi's home while he slept. They used an advanced EEG imaging system along with Apple's new QuickTime 8.0 beta with Brain2Vid technology to capture the movie. Pirates then edited out the unnecessary portions of what they captured, such as images of Raimi's mother yelling at him because he forgot to take out the garbage.

Raimi has confirmed that this is indeed the movie he is about to film. "I knew I shouldn't think about what I'm going to film. Now it's loose on the Internet. I'm just really glad I didn't have that goat dream."

"This is outrageous," said MPAA president Dan Glickman, "These criminals, by posting the film on the Internet before it has been released, are not only stealing revenue from the producers but also ruining the moviegoers' magical ringtone-filled experience at the theater."

According to one Internet research firm, the film was downloaded over 700,000,000 times in less than fourteen hours and will cost the studio at least $5 trillion in lost revenue. "We stand by our numbers even if they might seem a tad exaggerated. We really need the press," a representative for the firm said.

The Lord
of the Rings

Geek Cred: J. R. R. Tolkien's
The Lord of the Rings is the
fantasy novel to which all
others are compared. The
three-volume work follows
the adventures of the Hobbit
Frodo and his journey
through Middle Earth to
destroy Sauron's one ring
of power.

Geek Facts:

- Awarded the International Fantasy Award in 1957.
- Inspiration for Dungeons and Dragons, Nethack, and other geek games.
- Tolkein originally envisioned Frodo with an 18" Afro, but couldn't figure out how to fit it into the mythology of Hobbits.
- Glorfindel was the only Elf from Middle-earth who worked for Santa, according to notes never discovered in the margins of Tolkein's original manuscripts.
- If you start Pink Floyd's *Dark Side of the Moon* album as soon as you start reading Chapter 2 of *The Fellowship of the Ring,* you'll find many eerie coincidences.
- Like Hobbits, Tolkien ate six times a day while writing the book. Unlike the Hobbits, he ate small children.

Top 11 Characters Tolkien Removed from the Final Manuscript of *The Lord of the Rings*

11. Leagol—Gollum's twin brother, a lawyer who sued Gollum for custody of the ring.

10. Glorfunkel—A balding, less attractive cousin of Glorfindel nobody really cared for.

9. Gaydalf—The happiest wizard in Middle-earth, he wore rainbow-colored robes.

8. Mauron—The half-witted half brother of Sauron, whom Tolkien used as comic relief in Mordor.

7. Ropo "The Razor" Bulger—Notorious killer of Hobbit children.

6. Flaz-Rak—Saruman's Uruk-hai concubine.

5. Benito Mussolini—Haradrim leader who cozied up to Sauron.

4. Floin—Dwarf gangster rap star known for dope rhymes and addiction to pipeweed.

3. Nutsack—An Ent who used the giant nuts that grow on his branches to bring down the walls at Isengard.

2. Harry Potter—Teenage human wizard charged with defeating the evil Sauron.

1. The Nuzzles—The soft cuddly cousins of the Nazgul.

Manga

Geek Cred: It's hard to walk through the comics aisle of a bookstore without tripping over a manga geek. Manga is the Japanese word for comic. Manga comes in all different flavors from children's work to porn, and everything in between.

Geek Facts:

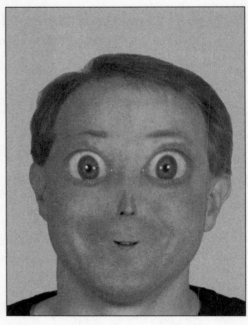

- A "mangaka" is the Japanese word for the author or artist of manga.

- You can blame Osamu Tezuka for the "large eye" style of many manga.

- The name manga comes from American G.I.s after World War II, who said the character's eyes looked like mangos. The Japanese thought they heard "manga," and the name stuck.

- Manga is read by all ages, due to a Japanese law forbidding any books other than manga.

- Since 1995, Pikachu has appeared in every manga released in Japan.

- Manga is so respected in Japan that members of parliament regularly dress up as their favorite manga characters during visits from foreign dignitaries.

Evolutionary Effects of Manga Makes
Japanese Eyes Bigger

TOKYO, JAPAN – Researchers at the University of Tokyo have studied photographs, and doctors' records to compare eye size of Japanese people
from today to people fifty years ago. They have found that eyes are 15
percent larger and trace it to the evolutionary effects of manga.

In Japan, more than 90 percent of people regularly read manga.
Higochi Sutochi, who was lead researcher on the study, said, "By looking
at the larger-than-life eyes of manga characters, readers subconsciously
move muscles that cause a genetic trigger to kick in and cause larger
eyes in offspring. If this trend continues, all Japanese people will have the
saucerlike eyes familiar to many manga fans."

Mangaka (manga artists) have responded by making manga characters' eyes even larger. This could lead to ridiculous proportions in characters whose eyes are physically larger than their heads.

Walter Dervish, a research biologist at Harvard, said, "Something may
have been lost in translation in the study. I don't really think that reading
comics causes people's eyes to get bigger, though reading Hemingway
does make your brain bigger."

Sutochi had no idea why only the eyes grew larger, and noses and
mouths did not grow smaller. "Maybe it only works on making things bigger," he said.

In response to the study, many Japanese men have asked artists to
draw bigger bulges on manga characters in hope the effect also works on
other areas.

X-Men

Geek Cred: *The X-Men* is a comic book about a group of mutant superheroes. It was created by Stan Lee and Jack Kirby in 1963. Like many geeks, mutants are shunned by society because they are different.

Geek Facts:

- Wolverine, the most popular mutant, made his first appearance in *The Incredible Hulk*.

- The original name for the comic was *The Mutants*.

- Feminist activists forced Marvel to rename the comic *X-Myn* for a short period of time in the 1990s.

- In *X-Men Adventures* #14, Wolverine escapes capture from Magneto by passing gas in an elevator.

- The strict Comics Code prevented Stan Lee and Jack Kirby from including Mangina and Bitchslapper as mutants.

- Patrick Stewart was chosen to play the role of Dr. X for the movies because he is telepathic in real life.

Top 11 Unlikely X-Men

11. Barfsop—Able to soak up small beverage spills and vomit.

10. Mastermind—Uses ESP to guess the order and colors of the enemy's ammo.

9. Retina—Has the ability to shoot his eyeballs from their sockets.

8. Hotdog—Can chew up various meat by-products and excrete edible sausages.

7. Sprinkle—Creates a mildly annoying mist at will.

6. Freedom—Her body adjusts to fit comfortably into any clothing.

5. Triclops—Third eye really freaks out his enemies.

4. Catheter—Strawlike fingers helpful for draining fluids.

3. Thermic—His hands can make things room temperature.

2. Translucid—Can almost become invisible.

1. Osmosis—Cannot get the crap beat out of him, because he has no bowels.

Dune

Geek Cred: Frank Herbert's *Dune* is the best-selling science fiction novel of all time, with over twelve million in sales. Set roughly 20,000 years in the future, the novel tells the story of the desert planet Arrakis, which is the source for the most valuable substance in the universe, the spice mélange.

got sand?

Geek Facts:

- *Dune* won the Nebula Award for best novel in 1965 and the Hugo Award for best novel in 1966.

- George Lucas has credited *Dune* as a major influence on the *Star Wars* trilogies.

- Herbert created many of the new words in *Dune* by using anagrams. For example Muad'Dib is Dumb Aid and the Bene Gesserit is from Big Tree Sense.

- Herbert was heavily inspired by the song "Remember (Walking in the Sand)" by the Shangri-Las when writing *Dune*.

- When talking about the symbolism in *Dune,* Herbert said, "Sometimes riding on the back of a giant sandworm is just riding on the back of a giant sandworm."

- *Dune* is the official novel of the kingdom of Saudi Arabia and is required reading for all Arabian high school students.

Top 11 Signs Your Sandworm Is Too Big

11. It just ate your house.

10. You put it in the Sahara and it barely has space to move around.

9.   All the other sandworms call it "Longy."

8.   Nothing at the Big and Long Shop for Sandworms fits it.

7.   You had to kill five hundred cows to make its leather pet collar.

6.   The Fremen women are afraid of it.

5.   It causes sandstorms when it snores.

4.   People often mistake it for a mountain range.

3.   The Arrakis Triathlon involves running around it twice.

2.   The annual Fremen Rock Festival uses it for shade.

1.   Wes Craven has optioned the rights to do the story of its life.

O'Reilly Media

Geek Cred: O'Reilly Media is the leading publishing company of bleeding-edge technology books started by Tim O'Reilly in 1978. Their most famous series is the "animal books" for computer programming, which feature a picture of an animal for each programming language, like the camel for Perl.

Geek Facts:

- O'Reilly's conference division hosts over a dozen conferences every year.
- The founder of O'Reilly Media, Tim O'Reilly, is credited with coining the term Web 2.0. Please don't hold that against him.
- The first book on Visual Basic featured a woodcut of a pile of elephant dung on the cover.
- In his book *The Road Ahead,* Bill Gates credited the O'Reilly book *Creating a Software Monopoly in a Nutshell* with his success in business.
- The shortest book in the O'Reilly library is *Internet Explorer Tips and Tricks.* It has one page, which says "Use Firefox."
- The animal featured on the cover of the *Ajax on Rails* book is Harold, the Peruvian spider monkey, because he wrote the book.

Top 11 Computer Books You Don't Need

11. Teach Yourself Ruby on Rails in Three Centuries

10. Essential Perl for the AOLer

9.   Where's That Damn Manual: The Missing Manual

8.   HTML and XHTML: WTF Are They All About?

7.   Essential Blogging: Whining About Not Being Linked

6.   Python Cookbook and BBQ Guide

5.   The Things Your Mother Never Told You About SQL

4.   Mastering Regular Expressions to Impress the Ladies

3.   How to Cheat at Microsoft Solitaire

2.   Mastering the Chiclet Keyboard: Typing 80 WPM on the IBM PC Jr in 27 Days.

1.   Windows ME Nonannoyances

Web Comics

Geek Cred: The advent of the Internet allowed many aspiring comic artists to put their work online for the world to see. Most geeks have a list of comics they check on regularly. Web comics fill all genres and types from single panels to full graphic novels.

Geek Facts:

- *Doctor Fun* was the first comic on the Web. *Where the Buffalo Roam* was the first comic on the Internet (Usenet).

- The creator of the popular *xkcd* Web comic used to work on robots at NASA before doing his comic full-time.

- Even with popular sites getting millions of hits each month, the average Web comic only receives two page views each day.

- An animated Gabe and Tycho from *Penny Arcade* appeared at the halftime show of Super Bowl XL.

- To compete better with online comics, *Dilbert* creator Scott Adams began using the word "fuck" in his strips at least twice a week.

- Because of high-paying "shock the monkey" ads, the online comic industry generates more revenue than all the Hollywood movie studios combined.

T-shirt image is courtesy of xkcd.com.

Microsoft Releases MS Paint Comic Edition for Vista

REDMOND, WA – Hoping to spur upgrades to Windows Vista, Microsoft has released MS Paint CE (Comics Edition) exclusively on Vista.

Lead MS Paint developer Justin Hans said, "We're excited to offer Web comic artists the premiere tool for comic development. The CE edition offers three new colors, improved gif compression and two more versions of Comic Sans, among others."

MS Paint CE resulted from years of research by Microsoft's Advance Comic Imaging Group. "We spent years studying the needs of Web comic artists and this is the perfect tool for them," said Hans

Randall Munroe of xkcd.com was excited by the news. "Until now I've been using a random image generator for my comics. MS Paint CE looks like the way to go."

"Since most Web comics are created in MS Paint, and there are over 40 million Web comics on the Internet, this could be the killer app that Vista has needed," said Christine Telford from The Gartner Group.

MS Paint CE also features a story line generation tool, an improved square tool for panel creation, and 7X zoom. "Like the Zune, Vista, and the Xbox 360 warranty repair issue, we've got ourselves a winner," said Hans.

Other comic artists weren't convinced. Mike Krahulik, of the popular *Penny Arcade* comic, said, "I'm taking a wait-and-see attitude. Until things play out, I'll stick with my goat's blood on stretched sheep's bladder."

GAMING

Chess

Geek Cred: Historically, the game most associated with geeks because of the deep strategies and creativity needed to win. Many geeks didn't know who to root for when IBM created Deep Blue, a chess-playing computer, to compete against Garry Kasparov. Deep Blue won.

Geek Facts:

- Lewis Carroll's a bit of a geek himself. *Through the Looking-Glass* is loosely based on a chess game.
- Bobby Fischer was the only American chess champion (1972–1975) during the Soviet era.
- The Snooka Maneuver, a classic chess strategy, involves flipping over the chessboard and scattering the pieces, then pummeling your opponent with your chair.
- The current American champion is a four-year-old chimpanzee called Twinkles.
- Secretary of State William Seward beat Tsar Alexander II in a chess match in San Francisco. The prize for winning was the state of Alaska.
- Britney Spears is an avid chess player, and even knows how all the pieces move, except for the bishop.

Chess Federation Proposes Rule Changes

MOSCOW, RUSSIA – After the 1997 victory by IBM's Deep Blue computer against Grand Master Garry Kasparov, the International Chess Rules Organization (ICRO) started developing new rules to keep humans competitive against computers. The new rules will be implemented next year.

Simon Jagaroff, President of ICRO, said, "We can't have the game, which is a measure of human intelligence, dominated by computers. Right now, six of the top ten players in the world are computers. If the game doesn't change, it could soon be all ten."

The rules will level the playing field, and some think even eliminate computers from the competition. Here are a few of the new rules:

- When two pawns are taken in succession, both players will have to take a bite of a banana or other fruit, or lose their queen.

- If a player cannot provide a DNA sample, then that player's rooks will be limited to moving two spaces at a time for the entire match.

- A checkmate only becomes official after the winning player gives the official judge a "high five." Otherwise, the game is considered a draw.

As expected, human players welcomed the rule changes while computer players raised many protests.

Ravi Gajat said, "I'm tired of hunks of silicon beating me. Humans created chess for humans to play."

ChessMaster 2000XL said, "101010."

LEGO

Geek Cred: LEGO bricks are the building blocks of geekdom. The bricks are made by the Denmark-based LEGO Group. Geeks love them because they foster imagination and creativity. Some decry LEGO's move into custom sets as stifling creativity, but no one would turn down a Millennium Falcon set.

Geek Facts:

- About 20 billion LEGO bricks are manufactured each year.

- Since 1958, all LEGO products are compatible no matter where or when they were made. The bricks you had as a kid will work with the ones you buy today.

- In 1972 the Pentagon commissioned a study to find out if it was possible to build fighting vehicles out of LEGO bricks. Many generals felt a LEGO fighting vehicle would give them maximum flexibility in combat.

- The largest structure ever built out of LEGO bricks was a life-size replica of the Sears Tower in Chicago in 1987.

- A cross-promotion with Kellogg's in the 1980s failed miserably when people refused to eat plastic waffles under the name of LEGO Eggo.

- In Denmark, the home of LEGO, a LEGO building contest is held every four years to determine who will be the next Prime Minister.

Top 11 Signs You Have Too Many LEGO Bricks

11. The spreadsheet you keep track of your LEGO sets on just ran out of rows.

10. You evict your kids from their room so you have somewhere to place your LEGO model of Manhattan.

9. You seriously considered doing the addition to your home in LEGO bricks.

8. You search the Internet hoping to find the "Nutrition Facts" for LEGO bricks.

7. There's a statue of you in every village in Denmark.

6. You know someone got up to use the bathroom in the middle of the night because you can hear their yelps of pain as they step on LEGO bricks you left lying around.

5. Three of your nephews went into the "LEGO room" two weeks ago, and haven't returned. You have to rent a backhoe to unearth them.

4. "LEGO sets" is the largest item in the family budget.

3. Your house is targeted by DHS for having Weapons of Mass Construction.

2. It's not uncommon to bite into a piece of homemade pie and find a LEGO brick that accidentally fell into the filling.

1. Your house burns down and all that's left is a molten lake of plastic.

Nintendo

Geek Cred: From Donkey Kong to the Wii, Nintendo is a gaming icon. The company has created the most popular gaming franchises "Mario" and "Pokémon" as well as the most popular handheld gaming system, the Game Boy. The NES was responsible for restarting the gaming industry after the crash of 1983.

Geek Facts:

- The original Super Mario Bros. is the biggest selling console game of all time.

- Universal City Studios, the owner of the King Kong trademark, sued Nintendo over Donkey Kong, but lost.

- Wii owners in Japan have been using superglue to attach Wii controllers to their hands, so the Wiimote doesn't fly away and damage their expensive televisions.

- The most popular name in Japan for boys is Mario; for girls it's Koopa.

- While Universal lost its lawsuit against Nintendo, the Ape Defamation League's suit was successful. The result was Donkey Kong Jr., in which the apes were portrayed as heroes.

- A recent study showed that nearly 95 percent of Internet humorists have made a urine joke about the Nintendo Wii.

Sony to Bundle Wii System with PS3 to Increase Sales

TOKYO – President of Sony North America, Frank Newmark, announced that Sony would begin bundling a Nintendo Wii console with every PlayStation 3 system sold.

Newmark hopes the new strategy will boost disappointing sales of the company's gaming system by pairing it with the hot-selling Wii. Newmark said, "By focusing on giving the customer what they want, the sales of the PS3 will improve dramatically."

Newmark confirmed that part of the strategy includes shifting manufacturing at one of Sony's plants from PS3s to Wii systems to meet the expected demand. "I know it sounds unorthodox to manufacture a competitor's product, but if you do the math, you'll see that it will help us increase market share," he said.

Many consumers were excited by the news. Thad Dorman of Oklahoma City said, "I've been trying to get my hands on a Wii since it came out. Now if I buy one direct from Sony, I get a PS3 in the bundle for less than I could've bought a Wii for by itself."

When asked what he would do with two consoles, Dorman answered, "I'll play the Wii and probably use the PS3 as a doorstop or something."

A representative for Nintendo confirmed the Sony plan and said that everyone at headquarters thought "the whole thing was pretty weird."

The PS3-Wii bundle will not increase the price of the PlayStation 3 system and will be available the beginning of April. Sony shares traded up on the Nikkei after the announcement.

Doom

Geek Cred: Doom, a first-person shooter, spawned many sequels and a movie starring The Rock. The game's 3D graphics and networked "deathmatches" made it a seminal game. Plenty of gore and Satanic imagery caused some controversy, but what do you expect when you open a portal to hell?

Geek Facts:

- Doom won multiple "Game of the Year" awards in 1994.

- The source code for Doom was released under GPL in 1999.

- NASA scientists required both Mars rovers to complete a run-through of Doom before they were allowed to leave Earth.

- Rumors have circulated that George W. Bush was an avid Doom player, and created levels of Saddam Hussein's palaces. This led to speculation that the game might be responsible for leading the United States into the second Gulf War.

- Doom was the first game to feature the Dremel rotary tool as a weapon.

- The story told in Doom is loosely based on the classic Ray Bradbury science fiction novel *Blowing Shit Away on Mars*.

Demon Spawn from Hell Sign Exclusive Deal with ID Software

SANTA MONICA, CA — Yorglock, President of United Demon Workers, and Carl Sanchez, CEO of Id Software, announced the two groups had signed an exclusive arrangement for featuring demons from hell in video games.

The deal prevents other companies from using "demons or likenesses of demons from hell in any computer, console or other video game," but does not cover demons from other locations, like alternate universes or Cleveland.

The agreement pleased rank-and-file members who spend most of their time strafed by chain guns and rocket launchers. "This guarantees work for me and my spawn in future Id releases, and ensures a quality death," said Elsnor the Tormentor. "Nothing upsets a demon more than some crappy rendering and choppy head explosions."

Yorglock cited popular games like Half-Life 2, which featured aliens from another world, as the main reason for striking the deal. "More game companies are finding cheap alien monsters to do the work that demons from hell have been doing. We may be more expensive than aliens or zombies, but we're worth it," said Yorglick.

Excruciate Software, a competing game producer, said the deal would prevent it from releasing Demon Hell Spawn 3, which it has re-named Alien Zombie Babies. Excruciate CEO Jordan Hampton said, "We're happy to be working with the alien zombie babies. Sure, we're disappointed we can't have demons from hell, but people just want to blow up monsters and don't care where they're from."

Gamer Tevin Golman echoed this sentiment while looking up from his Xbox 360, "I don't care where monsters come from, I just like blowing them up."

Id denied reports that the deal included a clause that would also shift some programming jobs to demon workers.

Rubik's Cube

Geek Cred: The Rubik's Cube is one of the best-selling toys in history, and it actually requires brains to solve. With 43 quintillion combinations, it's a geek badge of honor to have solved the cube at least once in a lifetime (without taking it apart with a screwdriver).

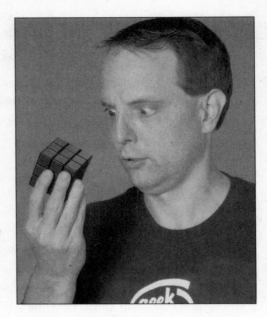

Geek Facts:

- A Saturday-morning cartoon series called *Rubik, the Amazing Cube* ran for one season on ABC in 1983.

- Cubes that are one, two, three, four, and five pieces wide have been released.

- In 2003 in Omaha, a parachute-pant-clad Michael J. Fox, high on cocaine, solved a Rubik's Cube while breakdancing and singing the theme from *Footloose,* causing space-time to warp and pulling the city back into the '80s.

- "Rubik's Wrist" was common among solvers because of repetitive motion used in solving the cube. Even more common was "Cube Head," caused by jocks smashing the cube in the forehead of the geek solving it.

- In *The Matrix,* Neo was supposed to solve a Rubik's Cube to save everyone, but Keanu Reeves could never do it, so they had him battle Agent Smith instead

- Rotating the right face once, the left face twice, and the bottom once causes the cube to enter a "cheat mode" from which it can be solved in only three moves.

Decline in Education Leads to Easier Cubes

TRENTON, NJ — While novelty cubes with only one color have been available for years, for the first time all Rubik's Cubes will be manufactured with only a single color, according to the Association of Rubik's Cube Manufacturers (ARCM).

"During the 1980s the Rubik's Cube was the puzzle that tested the smarts of kids and adults alike. That was the golden age of education. Cubes all contained a different color on each side. Things are different now," said Rex Plutoch, president of the ARCM.

"Cubes have seen a steady decline in difficulty. During the early '90s we switched to four-color cubes, then three, and finally in 2000 we started making dual-color cubes. This year all Rubik's Cubes will be manufactured with only a single color," said Plutoch.

Many see this change as a sign of the decline of the public educational system. "When I was a kid, the cube had quintillions of combinations. Now it only has one," said Bill Finster, a thirty-six-year-old math teacher in Pennsylvania. "Sadly even a cube like this might be too difficult for today's kids. Kids these days are used to only using their thumbs, so something like a cube that requires all your fingers might be too tough for them."

On the positive side, new world records for solving the new cube are being reported every day. "We've seen hundreds of competitors handing in sub-one-second times," said Valerie Shrum, who works for the *Guinness Book of World Records.*

Many parents appreciate the change. "My Tommy got very frustrated with the cube, so I'm glad they're switching to this version," said Margaret Brown, mother of two. "Now every kid can feel like a winner."

Plutoch said that all the challenge won't be removed from the cube. "We will offer different colored cubes; all yellow, all red, or all white. We haven't removed all the difficulty." Plutoch said that a prototype of a solid-colored cube with no moving parts was in the works for 2012.

First Video Game

Geek Cred: Like the "first computer," the first video game depends upon your definition of "video game." Table Tennis for Two on an oscilloscope, Spacewar on a PDP-1, Computer Space in the arcade, and the interactive TV game developed by Ralph Baer all have legitimate claims to this title.

Geek Facts:

- Though not the first video game, Pong did play an important part in bringing video games into the mainstream.

- The first video game home console was the Magnavox Odyssey.

- Tom Reynolds of Boston became the first person to put his fist through a video game display when he lost a Pong tournament in 1973.

- Early video games required players to hold joysticks that weighed over fifty pounds.

- The first adult video game was based on Pong and was called Dong.

- Nikola Tesla was the first person to develop a "radio game," but it was unplayable because, at the time, people couldn't see radio waves.

Top 11 Lessons Kids Can Learn
from Classic Arcade Games

11. People sometimes need food, badly.

10. If attacked by a pickle, sausage, or fried egg, be sure to have a pepper shaker handy.

 9. Bigger pills will give you more power

 8. It didn't take much to amuse kids in the '80s, and even less in the '70s.

 7. As long as the alligator's mouth is closed, it only takes one swipe of the knife to kill him. Otherwise, you're dead.

 6. Always watch out for falling spiders

 5. Asteroids are hollow and split in half if shot.

 4. When you're dead, you're dead. Life has no option to continue.

 3. Never trust a monkey with a barrel.

 2. How to make a statement with only three letters.

 1. If you're trapped underground, a pump isn't as worthless as it may seem.

LARP

Geek Cred: LARP stands for Live Action Role Playing. It's a game where geeks play the parts in an RPG like Dungeons and Dragons, but in a real-life environment. LARPs, like RPGs, span many genres from historical combat to modern-day espionage. Who said geeks don't get out much?

Lightning Bolt!

Geek Facts:

- It's hard to pinpoint the date of origin for LARPs, but it's around the late 1960s to early 1970s.

- Often a game of "Rock, Paper, Scissors" will determine who lives or dies.

- A Broadway play entitled "Magic Missile! Lightning Bolt!" broke the record for "longest-running play based on a LARP" after one performance.

- LARPs are so popular in Finland that August 3rd has been declared "National LARP Day" by the government, and all workers get a holiday.

- LARPers were successful in removing LARPing as a disease in the recent edition of the psychological disorders manual, *DSM-IV*.

- Natalie Portman is an avid LARPer and enjoys playing a half-orc assassin.

Thirty-two Arrested in Poorly Conceptualized LARP

WASHINGTON, D.C. – Police arrested thirty-two people after mistaking their live action role-playing (LARP) game for a terrorist plot.

Tommy Hopkins, who runs RPG Live Unlimited, the group that organized the game, said it may have been a bad idea to stage a terrorist genre LARP on the Capitol steps. "We needed a wide-open space near some government buildings to get more realism for the game, so this was a logical choice. But, in hindsight, maybe we should've chosen a medieval genre rather than a modern-day terrorist-counterterrorist game."

In a LARP, players assume the roles of the characters they play and then action is determined by a set of rules. In the game that resulted in arrests, the sixteen terrorists were supposed to plant a "bomb" on the steps of the Capitol building while the counterterrorists tried to stop them.

Despite pleas from the participants that they were just "playing a game," police arrested them and took them to jail.

"You can't just walk around the Capitol building dressed like an Al-Qaeda member carrying a fake bomb. That's against the law," said Police Chief Claude Barkins.

This wasn't the first incident of LARP players taking the game too far. Gamers in Sweden were arrested for practicing medicine without a license after performing a gallbladder surgery at a local hospital as part of a medical LARP.

Hopkins said the group's next game will probably have to take place in a prison environment. "It's a setting that doesn't come along often for us, but since we'll all be in there, we should take advantage of it."

Nethack

Geek Cred: A single-player dungeon exploration game entirely in ASCII characters that includes references to Tolkien, *Star Wars* and *The Hitchhiker's Guide to the Galaxy.* No save points, no extra lives. When you die, you're dead for good (unless you have that handy Amulet of Life Saving).

Geek Facts:

- The Quantum Mechanics in the game sometimes carry a box with Schrödinger's cat inside. Whether the cat is alive or dead is not determined until the box is opened.

- The first version of Nethack was posted to Usenet in 1987.

- Blizzard uses the Nethack engine to power an ASCII version of World of Warcraft for players still stuck with dial-up Internet access.

- The acronym YASD stands for "You're A Stupid Dog." Players yell this when their pet gets them killed.

- Playing an ASCII dungeon exploration game has been clinically proven to make you look better to the opposite sex.

- Some shopkeepers have lottery tickets. If you take off all your armor and zap them with a Wand of Striking, they will sell them to you.

New Card Pushes Limits of ASCII Gaming

MARKHAM, ON – The Nethack Devteam announced a new version of the popular text-based game, version 4.6.5. At the same press conference ATI announced a new video card, the ATI 3000-TXT, optimized for ASCII gaming.

"The VT100 standard has been around for years, but there hasn't been a video card company willing to make a card for it," said ATI Director of Product Development, Carlos Neale. "I think more card and gaming companies will jump on the text bandwagon now that we've thrown our support behind it."

Neale added that he felt that a frames-per-second (fps) rate of 1000 in Nethack was possible with the card.

The 3000-TXT has an added ASCII Processing Unit (APU) on the card to handle the complex calculations needed to render creatures like the A and the M in Nethack.

Hardcore text-gamers rejoiced at the news. Victor Harville, who runs ASCII-Gamer.com, a site dedicated to text-based games, was ecstatic. "I love this new card. The new Nethack takes advantage of the APU. I mean you haven't really Nethacked until you've passed the kHz barrier." Harville's review of the card was one word: "ASCIIcking!"

Dedicated Nethacker Byron Wilkes, who has ascended twelve times, said, "I was frightened when the band of o's attacked me. They were so realistically drawn. It was scary."

ATI also announced a card under development that would support Unicode gaming. "It's a real chicken-or-the-egg scenario. Do we make a card that supports Unicode gaming before there are games, or will the games appear after we make the card?"

Zork

Geek Cred: Zork was a
series of text-based adventure
games popular on early personal computer systems like
the Commodore 64, Apple II,
TRS-80, and Atari systems.
In the game, players used text
commands (more advanced
commands than any other
game of its time) to explore a
dungeon.

Geek Facts:

- "Zork" was a term to describe an incomplete program, but the name stuck.

- Zork I, II, and III are available for free download from Infocom.

- The grue was put on the endangered species list in 1992 after the rise of graphical adventure games destroyed much of its habitat.

- A group of twelve-year-old World of Warcraft players was unable to find its way into the White House after spending four hours playing Zork. They were seen jiggling the mouse many times.

- After the collapse of the Soviet Empire, the Eastern European nation of Ukraine adopted the Zorkmid as its national currency.

- Zork was one of the first games to have a cheat code. If you went N, S, N, W, S, N, you entered "God" mode and couldn't be eaten by a grue.

Grue Exhibit at Zoo Goes Horribly Wrong

SAN DIEGO, CA – Five people were killed and dozens injured when two grues escaped from their cage at the San Diego Zoo.

Long the nemesis of text adventure gamers everywhere, the grue now struggles to survive as its habitat has been destroyed by graphical adventure games. The grue exhibit at the San Diego Zoo was supposed to kick off a traveling exhibition called Getting Down with the Grue, which would bring exposure to the plight of the near-extinct grue.

"Because of their fear of light and their propensity for slaughter, most people have never actually seen a grue more than once," said zoo director Barry Plugh. "For the exhibition, we had infrared lights installed and patrons would don infrared goggles to see the grues. It would've been cool."

Plugh fears this terrible tragedy will decrease any public support for putting the grue on the endangered-species list.

Surviving zoo patrons agree. "Why would we want it to survive? Its only purpose is to lurk in the dark and kill us," said Debbie Kringle, who narrowly escaped.

Damien Hesse, who escaped the grue only because it was busy eating his friend, said, "I couldn't see much except for the slavering fangs. I was lucky to get out of there alive."

Grues are thought to be extinct in the wild, and only forty-two are left in captivity in zoos around the world. The traveling exhibition has been put on hold until further notice.

Pac-Man

Geek Cred: The iconic video game of the 1980s. Pac-Man gave rise to many game sequels, breakfast cereal, animated series, a board game, and many other creations. Many publications have rated it as the #1 video game of all time.

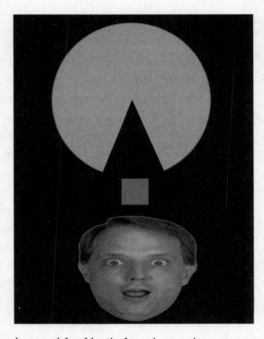

Geek Facts:

- The game was originally called *Puck Man* in Japan, but was changed for North American release.

- A perfect score in Pac-Man is 3,333,360 without losing a life and was first achieved in 1999.

- Short on ideas, one Hollywood studio has planned a live-action Pac-Man movie starring Colin Farrell and Jessica Biel.

- Many researchers attribute the rise in binge eating among Americans to the popularity of Pac-Man in the 1980s.

- Even in video games, women earn less than men. Ms. Pac-Man only cost 20 cents to play, compared to Pac-Man's quarter.

- Inky, Blinky, Pinky, and Clyde were named after the members of the Motown group The Four Tops.

Pac-Man Banned from Las Vegas Buffets

LAS VEGAS, NV — Classic arcade star Pac-Man has been banned from Las Vegas buffet restaurants after a nonstop binge at several of the establishments. Most people are familiar with Vegas-wide blacklists for card counters, but few know about the blacklist for buffets.

"I knew his reputation as an eater, but I didn't expect him to wipe out the entire buffet. It's not fair to the other patrons of the restaurant that he gets to eat everything," said Carl Gallian, manager of the buffet at Circus Circus. "I called around to some of the other managers and he had hit them, too. That's when we decided to put him on the list."

Pac-Man's entry on the list included several aliases Pac-Man uses, as well a picture of his trademark yellow head. "He can try to use a different name, or put on glasses and a wig, but that missing-slice-of-pizza yellow head is pretty distinct," said Gallian.

Pac-Man, who now headlines a musical revue entitled *Classic Aracadiarama* at the Monte Carlo, made his fortune from licensing his likeness during the 1980s arcade boom and remains a popular figure in gaming. Pac-Man said, "You'd think a big wheel like me could get comped at any buffet, but that's not the case. I'm pac-manna non gratis at these places. Fame just doesn't get you as far as it used to."

Gallian added, "He's welcome to eat at any of our other establishments, but I don't think that all-you-can-eat is ever going to happen for him. He's a bottomless pit."

Several bars in the area also banned Pac-Man from "quarter beer" night for similar reasons. Pac-Man said he would find a way to get his fill. "They can't stop me, I'm an eating machine."

Dungeons and Dragons

Geek Cred: Before computer graphics got good enough to display realistic blood, parents feared Dungeons and Dragons (D & D). That's a testament to the power and popularity of this open-ended role playing game created by Gary Gygax and Dave Arneson. It has spawned movies, books, toys, and an animated cartoon series.

Geek Facts:

- The first D & D tournament happened in 1976.

- Tom Hanks starred in the "scare-the-parents" TV movie called *Mazes and Monsters,* in which he kills his friends because he's obsessed with a D & D-type game.

- The longest-running game of D & D started in 1978 and still continues today.

- D & D players in the 1980s would commit suicide by jamming four-sided dice into their eye sockets after their characters died.

- Research shows that D & D players are not socially awkward and have more sexual relations with orc women than the general population.

- Most people think Paris Hilton spends her time in Manhattan hot spots drinking and dancing. In reality she's in a booth with her friends assaulting the Towers of Arcanexo with her level-26 paladin.

Top 11 Rejected Dungeons and Dragons
Character Classes

11. Nucleonic—A master of the nuclear arts. Can set off tactical nuclear strikes at will. Too overpowered.

10. Scarfwraith—A spectral warrior who is master of scarf combat.

9. Foodmancer—Master of competitive food eating. Very useful against black puddings. Can create hot dogs at will.

8. Interpretive Dancer—Flamboyant and theatrical, he does well to distract the enemies. Pairs well with Bards.

7. Rockstar—Has fast fingers, but has a tendency to drink too much and destroy dungeons.

6. Order of Odor—Expert at scent generation.

5. Pedopriest—Likes working with children.

4. Republican—Likes battles, but doesn't like to get involved in the melee.

3. Thymesage—Skilled with spices, but that's about it.

2. Barcodess—Gifted in labeling, but the technology to read them hasn't been developed yet.

1. Whackmaster—Master of whacking anything off.

Atari 2600

Geek Cred: Released in 1977, it wasn't the first gaming console, but it brought home video gaming to the masses. Separating the software from the hardware by putting games on cartridges allowed developers more freedom, and gave gamers more choices.

Geek Facts:

- Over 30 million Atari 2600 consoles were sold worldwide.

- The Atari 2600 was powered by the MOS Technology 6507 processor and ran at a blazing 1.19 MHz.

- Studies show that many children's lives were ruined when their parents chose to purchase a game system other than an Atari 2600.

- The computer graphics for the movie *TRON* were done entirely on a Beowulf cluster of Atari 2600s.

- Today, the design for the Atari 2600 joysticks is being used to produce sex toys in the Asian market.

- A charity called "Atari for Africa" puts used 2600 systems in the hands of poor children in Africa. Unfortunately, without food or electricity, most of the children die of starvation before being able to play the console.

E.T. Sequel Based on Atari 2600 Game Planned

HOLLYWOOD, CA—Steven Spielberg is in discussion with Atari about directing a sequel to *E.T. The Extraterrestrial* based on the Atari video game from 1982. The tentative title is *ET 2: Escape from the Wells.*

Spielberg said the project came about from the near success of other video-game-to-movie projects.

"This is a unique situation," said Spielberg. "This would be the first movie based on an Atari 2600-era console game. Also, it'd be the first movie based on a game based on a movie ever produced. I couldn't believe it hadn't been thought of before."

The script isn't complete, but Spielberg shared some of his thoughts. "It's set thirty years in the future. Global warming has caused a shortage of water, and rogue well-diggers roam the countryside digging dangerous wells without any safety precautions.

"Kids are falling into the wells and there aren't enough skilled people to save them. Elliott, now an environmental engineer, contacts E.T. and tells him of the problem. E.T. returns and uses his powers of levitation to save children and himself, after he gets stuck in the mud, from the dangerous wells."

Critics wonder what Spielberg is smoking. "Sure, the retrogaming fad is big among the Generation X crowd, but why choose one of the worst games ever?" said one critic. "Wouldn't *Pitfall!* Or *Kaboom!* make more sense? I mean they both have exclamation marks!"

Henry Thomas and Drew Barrymore have committed to reprise their roles for the film.

World of Warcraft

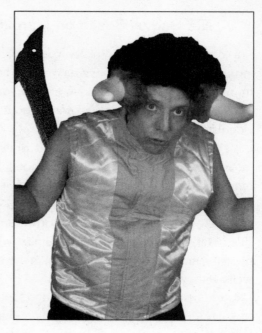

Geek Cred: The most popular of all massively multiplayer online role-playing games (MMORPG). Plenty of reference to other geek culture icons like an NPC named Linken (Link from Zelda games) and gorillas that drop empty barrels (Donkey Kong). World of Warcraft has eaten billions of hours from the lives of geeks.

Geek Facts:

- China has imposed limits on how long players can play online games to combat addiction to World of Warcraft.

- A *World of Warcraft* movie based on the game is in the works.

- The IRS has been considering accepting World of Warcraft gold for tax payments, so they can begin taxing in-game transactions.

- A murloc in the Redridge Mountains will drop a "Potion of Gain Level," but the drop rate is ridiculously low.

- If Kalimdor was rotated 90 degrees, it would be a perfect topographical match to the island of Manhattan.

- A giant meteor is heading toward Azeroth that will annihilate the entire continent in a "world-destroying event" in 2009. This will force many millions to return to their real lives.

Blizzard Selling LifePacks for Scheduled Downtime in World of Warcraft

IRVINE, CA – Blizzard Entertainment has begun selling LifePacks for the popular MMORPG World of Warcraft. LifePacks give the player a chance to experience life away from the World of Warcraft by causing scheduled downtime for accounts.

"We expect most LifePacks will be bought by someone other than the player, like spouses, parents, and girlfriends, to get some time with the player outside Azeroth," said Blizzard Entertainment representative Paul Vinton.

Vinton explained, "To the player, it will look like a standard server outage. We don't want to cause any conflicts and since server outages are common, the player won't suspect anything."

"I was beginning to wonder why the server always went down when we had to go to Aunt Doreen's. Now I know my parents have been buying LifePacks for me," said Chad Binghamton, a player on the Arthas server.

Not all LifePacks will be purchased by people other than the player. "We expect some players to buy the cards," said Vinton. "Say you've got a big test coming up and want to make sure that you have time to study for it. Buy a LifePack, and the server will be down, giving you time to study."

Gaming reporter Brian Keith said, "This is a genius marketing ploy by Blizzard; not only do you have to pay them to play the game, but now they'll be getting money for you to not play the game."

Civilization

Geek Cred: A turn-based strategy game developed by gaming legend Sid Meier. Civilization is one of those games that cause geeks to miss sleep, classes, and even work. Players develop a civilization and compete with other civilizations for world dominance. Sequels to the game have continued its popularity since its release in 1991.

Geek Facts:

- *Computer Gaming World* chose Civilization as the #1 game of all time in 1996.

- Sid Meier was the second person inducted into the Academy of Interactive Arts and Sciences' Hall of Fame

- A movie based on the game was filmed in 1997, but was never released because it was fifty-seven hours long.

- In 1992 the American Medical Association rated Civilization as "the second most addictive substance known to mankind behind crack cocaine."

- Civilization VI will be tied into Pentagon computer systems and allow players to control actual military units.

- In the French versions of the game, players were required by law to choose France as their starting Civilization.

Top 11 Signs You've Been Playing This Game of Civilization Too Long

11. Your computer starts begging for mercy.

10. Actual civilizations have risen and fallen while you've been playing.

9. The game has updated to a new version twice while you're playing.

8. You start as George Washington, but end as Chelsea Clinton's great-granddaughters.

7. You are researching Future Technology 829.

6. You call your kids worker units.

5. You've developed a pathological fear of axemen.

4. You're producing more food than the planet Earth.

3. "Having to fight off a Roman invasion" seems like a valid excuse for being late for work.

2. You didn't have a ten-inch beard when you sat down.

1. When you get up to walk, you can only take two steps at a time.

Half-Life

Geek Cred: Half-Life is often considered the best game of all time. The main character is Gordon Freeman, a theoretical physicist and research associate at the Black Mesa Laboratory. A mod for Half-Life became Counter-Strike.

Geek Facts:

- Half-Life and expansions all had scientific terms as titles: Half-Life, Opposing Force, and Blue Shift.

- Black Mesa's motto is: Working to build a better tomorrow for all mankind. So much for that.

- After graduate school, Gordon Freeman was deciding between a job at Black Mesa and Microsoft. He chose Black Mesa, because of the better retirement plan, and his love of train rides.

- If you talk to the manager at the Red Lobster in Avon, Utah, he can hook you up with a plate of fried headcrabs. They are very tasty with a squeeze of lemon.

- Instead of alien invaders, Valve originally wanted hordes of Rainbow Brite Color Kids, but were unable to secure a license from Hallmark.

- The expansion G-Force allowed players to play the G-man, but was considered too boring, because all he did was walk around with a briefcase.

Valve to Focus Exclusively on Elite Gamers

BELLVUE, WA — Valve plans on focusing on the elite few who can afford the latest in bleeding-edge hardware—and who are willing to pay a premium for quality games.

In a press release, Shawn Trail explained the bold move: "The market is full of middle-of-the-road companies that cater to Joe Average and his crappy old Dell. We're in the market to make games, not to waste our time on minimum and recommended settings. Who do you think has the most fun, the engineers at Kia or Lamborghini?"

The upper-class gaming market has become increasingly interesting lately because of the revival of the dot-com industry and resulting rise of rich nerds. By focusing on this group of consumers, Valve hopes to corner the market. Industry analyst Vincent Gustin welcomes the move: "We've been waiting for one of the big players to make the switch. It's not a big surprise that Valve was the first, but it's impressively bold of them to make a jump like this instead of adopting a dual-market strategy."

Many gamers applauded the move. "I want to assure that I'm playing these online games with other investment bankers, or at least the kids of investment bankers," said Willie Pink, a gaming enthusiast at Merrill Lynch.

Valve plans to release periodic mandatory updates through Steam to keep the games only playable by bleeding-edge systems. Competitor Ubisoft said they were looking for ways to make their games more difficult to install to keep pace with Valve.

Pokémon

Geek Cred: Pokémon targets younger geeks and prepares them for a life of gaming. It's a card game, a video game, a TV series, a series of movies, and just about anything else you can imagine. The Pokémon games for the Nintendo Game Boy are some of the best-selling games ever.

Geek Facts:

- A Pokémon cartoon caused several hundred children to have seizures in Japan.

- Over 150 million Pokémon video games have been sold worldwide.

- The film *Pokémon Heroes* caused several hundred critics to vomit.

- Gregathor is the most powerful Pokémon and is unbeatable except by Metapod.

- In the card game, in case of a tie, players throw cards at one another until the loser bleeds.

- At the Nintendo-run Pokémon University in Japan, Pokétrainers can earn degrees in Pokemonology and economics.

Pokémon, Yu-Gi-Oh, or Drug Slang?

Can you tell which term is a Pokémon, a Yu-Gi-Oh card, or drug slang?

1.	Barboach	Pokémon	Yu-Gi-Oh	Drug Slang
2.	Great White	Pokémon	Yu-Gi-Oh	Drug Slang
3.	Electabuzz	Pokémon	Yu-Gi-Oh	Drug Slang
4.	Golden Dragon	Pokémon	Yu-Gi-Oh	Drug Slang
5.	Shroomish	Pokémon	Yu-Gi-Oh	Drug Slang
6.	Killer Needle	Pokémon	Yu-Gi-Oh	Drug Slang
7.	Weedle	Pokémon	Yu-Gi-Oh	Drug Slang
8.	Barrel Dragon	Pokémon	Yu-Gi-Oh	Drug Slang
9.	Zigzagoon	Pokémon	Yu-Gi-Oh	Drug Slang
10.	Whiffenpopper	Pokémon	Yu-Gi-Oh	Drug Slang
11.	Magical Ghost	Pokémon	Yu-Gi-Oh	Drug Slang
12.	Nosepass	Pokémon	Yu-Gi-Oh	Drug Slang
13.	Hero of the Underworld	Pokémon	Yu-Gi-Oh	Drug Slang
14.	Doma the Angel of Silence	Pokémon	Yu-Gi-Oh	Drug Slang
15.	Bambalacha	Pokémon	Yu-Gi-Oh	Drug Slang
16.	Drooling Lizard	Pokémon	Yu-Gi-Oh	Drug Slang

MOVIES

Star Wars: Episode V— The Empire Strikes Back

Geek Cred: Considered by geeks to be the best of the movies in the *Star Wars* trilogies. Coincidentally, it's the only *Star Wars* movie not directed by George Lucas, but instead by Irvin Kershner. Has one of the most memorable lines in movie history with Darth Vader's, "No, I am your father."

Geek Facts:

- *The Empire Strikes Back* was the highest-grossing film of 1980.

- The *Millennium Falcon* was built for the first and only time for this installment.

- Han could've avoided the trap in Cloud City if he had only listened to Admiral Ackbar.

- The original script called for Leia to wear a fur-lined bikini on Hoth, but the cold weather caused constant "headlight" problems.

- Mark Hamill never realized Yoda was a puppet until watching the "Making of *Star Wars*" documentary. All along he thought Yoda was a mutant child.

- Lucas financed *The Empire Strikes Back* with lottery winnings.

Star Wars Character or Hip-Hop Artist?

Can you tell which of these is a character from the *Star Wars* universe and which is a hip-hop artist?

1.	Luke Skyywalker	*Star Wars*	Hip-Hop
2.	Droopy McCool	*Star Wars*	Hip-Hop
3.	Sly Moore	*Star Wars*	Hip-Hop
4.	Talib Kweli	*Star Wars*	Hip-Hop
5.	Mawhonic	*Star Wars*	Hip-Hop
6.	Boss Nass	*Star Wars*	Hip-Hop
7.	Obie Trice	*Star Wars*	Hip-Hop
8.	Phoenix Orion	*Star Wars*	Hip-Hop
9.	Jasper McKnives	*Star Wars*	Hip-Hop
10.	Sly Boogy	*Star Wars*	Hip-Hop
11.	Anchor Blue	*Star Wars*	Hip-Hop
12.	Mabulu	*Star Wars*	Hip-Hop
13.	Mangu	*Star Wars*	Hip-Hop
14.	Rappertunie	*Star Wars*	Hip-Hop
15.	Joh Yowza	*Star Wars*	Hip-Hop
16.	Kit Fisto	*Star Wars*	Hip-Hop

Blade Runner

Geek Cred: This movie sets the standard by which most modern science fiction films are judged. Based on the Philip K. Dick novel *Do Androids Dream of Electric Sheep?*, the movie deals with questions of creation and what constitutes life.

Geek Facts:

- The title of the film comes from a book by Alan Nourse, though the film has nothing to do with the book.

- The movie won the Hugo Award in 1983 for Best Dramatic Presentation.

- *Blade Runner II: The Honeymoon* with Harrison Ford reprising his role as the android hunter-cum-lover is in pre-production and is scheduled to be released in 2009.

- So many different cuts were made of the film that Ridley Scott called in DJ Jazzy Jeff to help.

- After screening the film for a group of senators, a bill was introduced called the Android Protection Act, but it never made it out of committee.

- Harrison Ford said this was his favorite role "right after all the other ones."

Extras Cut of *Blade Runner* Planned

HOLLYWOOD, CA – Alan Drexler, President of Warner Home Video, announced that another cut of the classic science fiction film *Blade Runner,* The Extras Cut, will be released later this year.

Several cuts of the film have already been released theatrically and on video, including the Director's Cut, an International Cut, and 2007's falsely named Final Cut. Drexler said, "*Blade Runner* has a long legacy of different versions. We felt it was imperative to continue that tradition."

This version of the film was put together by a group of five extras who played various roles in the film. Clarence Cho, who played the "Guy with Ostriches," said, "I loved my experience on *Blade Runner,* so I was happy to contribute to the artistry. I sell insurance now, so learning film editing was difficult, but worth it. Now, instead of being on screen for a mere two seconds, I'm up there for nearly five minutes. I think it really adds to the film."

The Extras Cut lasts forty-five minutes and consists mostly of scenes featuring the extras. "I think the extras really bring texture to the story, so by focusing on them, people get a better feeling of what it will be like in 2019," said Bill Xiao, who played "Guy in Bar" in the Director's Cut, but was cut out of the Final Cut.

"The shorter length and the focus on the chaotic street scenes should give the film a broader appeal than the original which many people, including me, consider too 'thinky,' " said Drexler. "Even if this version isn't successful, we're still planning the Dolly Grip Cut in 2009 and the Craft Service Worker Cut in 2010."

Director Ridley Scott made no comment on the upcoming versions, but just wept softly in a corner. *Blade Runner: The Extras Cut* will be available in December 2008.

Metropolis

Geek Cred: *Metropolis* was a groundbreaking silent science fiction film directed by Fritz Lang that still influences modern cinema. The story had innovative special effects, a humanoid robot, and a mad scientist wearing a glove on only one hand: everything a geek film needs.

Geek Facts:

- Sadly, over a quarter of the original film has been lost.

- The movie cost roughly 200 million dollars to produce in today's dollars.

- George Lucas had plans to release *Star Wars* as a silent film, which led to the opening text scrolling of each film, but scrapped plans when he realized it was a dumb idea.

- During screenings of the film in Germany in 1927, audiences were so frightened by lifelike robots that they started planning the invasion of Poland.

- A lip reader was employed to see what the actors were actually saying in the film. Strangely, all of them just kept repeating "Schieß auf das fenster."

- Michael Jackson owns the original "Maria" robot costume, and likes to put it on and do the moonwalk.

Top 11 Signs Your Boss Might Be an Evil Robot

11. He puts cream and "Chronox's Robo Lubricant" into his coffee.

10. Instead of "casual Fridays," your company has "show your metal" Mondays.

9. He never goes to the bathroom.

8. The whirring sound right before he shoots lasers from his eyes.

7. You catch her dancing at the German burlesque show down at the Metropolis Bar.

6. He talks into the phone with a high-pitched squealing sound.

5. Never once stops to play solitaire or minesweeper.

4. Can do "the robot" but can't do "the wave."

3. Wears a goatee-shaped magnet.

2. He mentions how he thinks the robots got the shaft in all the Terminator movies.

1. She asks you to join her robot insurrection group.

The Day the Earth Stood Still

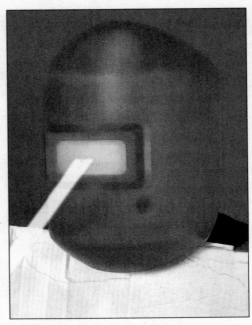

Geek Cred: It's a simple science fiction story. Alien comes to Earth. Panicked Earthlings shoot alien ten seconds after he leaves his ship. His indestructible robot frightens everyone. In the end, he tells earth to "stop fighting, or we'll blow your planet up," and leaves.

Geek Facts:

- The guy who played Gort was too weak to carry anybody, so wires were needed to hold the people when he was "carrying" them.

- Twenty-eight years later, the director, Robert Wise, also directed another geek favorite: *Star Trek: The Motion Picture.*

- After the premiere of the film many people thought Michael Rennie, the actor who played Klaatu, was an alien and tried to shoot him.

- The film prompted the U.S. Army to change their policy on "first contact" with an alien species. Instead of "shooting first and asking questions later," the army would be sure to "shoot to kill" and forget about the questions.

- Censors forced a redesign of Gort's helmet, as they deemed the original design to be too phallic, especially in the scene where he uses his head to pleasure Helen.

- While this film is tame by today's standards, audiences in the 1950s had to be given health warnings because of the nonstop action.

Top 11 Things Not to Say to an Indestructible Killer Robot

11. I bet that shoulder-mounted laser cannon can't shoot a hole through my skull.

10. That stupid toaster brother of yours burnt my toast again this morning.

9. Yeah, I'm John Connor. Who wants to know?

8. Clapper Secada Licktoes.

7. Hey, aren't you that indestructible killer robot that the robot police are looking for?

6. I knew Gort. I worked with Gort. You sir, are no Gort.

5. You kind of remind me of Johnny 5.

4. What robot does a guy have to lubricate around here to get decapitated?

3. Does that eye-beam do anything useful, or is it just there to make you look pretty?

2. Ha-ha, you can't hurt me. Don't you know about Asimov's Laws of Robotics?

1. I heard that you and C-3P0 were like, doing it.

2001: A Space Odyssey

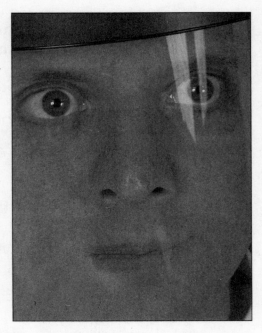

Geek Cred: The movie deals with topics dear to any geek's heart: technology, artificial intelligence, evolution, and space. The film is praised for its scientific accuracy compared to most space films, though it is not perfectly accurate.

Geek Facts:

- Douglas Rain, who was the voice of HAL, never set foot on the movie set.

- If you shift the letters of HAL by one letter you get IBM, though Clarke claimed this was unintentional.

- One glaring scientific error in the film occurs when we see the ape-man using the bone to kill his buddy. Everyone knows the first tool used by man to kill his buddy was a rock.

- If the United States decides to launch nuclear missiles, the computer will tell them "I'm sorry Dave, I'm afraid I can't do that," because of a joke program put in by contractors who were big fans of the film.

- A dance number featuring Bowman and the dead astronauts was cut from the U.S. release of the film.

- The film ranked #8 in the American Film Institute's list of Top 100 Least Understood Films.

Top 11 Signs You Shouldn't Board That Spacecraft

11. The computer's name is HAL Jr.

10. Your lips are easy to read.

9. The captain insists you put on a red shirt before you board the ship.

8. It's a COOKBOOK!

7. It comes with preinstalled gremlins on the wings.

6. The logo on the side is a huge, black monolith.

5. The captain asks if you've got any dilithium crystals he can borrow.

4. It's abandoned in the middle of space and there's valuable cargo on board that your greedy captain wants to get his hands on.

3. It lists the entertainment as "Vogon Poetry Readings."

2. It says it's heading for Alderaan.

1. A Dr. Smith is listed on the passenger manifest.

Monty Python and the Holy Grail

Geek Cred: It would be hard to go a full day in any geek workplace without some reference to *Holy Grail,* whether it be "It's just a flesh wound" or "Run away!" Python's influence on geek culture is broad as well, from "spam" to the Python programming language, but this movie is their crown jewel.

Geek Facts:

- Pink Floyd and Led Zeppelin invested money to get the movie made.

- Terry Gilliam dies four times in the movie, more than any other Python.

- Not knowing how to do special effects, the Pythons had John Cleese amputate his arms and legs for the "Black Knight" scenes. They were reattached at the end of the day.

- The scenes where sunlight is visible were shot in France.

- Colin Powell, a big fan of Monty Python, when making a case for the invasion of Iraq, told the United Nations that Saddam Hussein could be breeding "killer rabbits like those in *Holy Grail.*"

- The "Knights Who Say Ni" were originally supposed to be a Mormon rock group, but that was considered too silly and the scene was changed.

Geek's Monty Python Report Earns a Beating

MONROEVILLE, PA – High school Senior Jared Blanks was surprised that he earned a beating from the "cool kids" with his report on the many humorous quotes from Monty Python.

"Usually it's just some teasing, or maybe a punch in the shoulder, but this time it was a downright beating. I got a bloody lip and everything. I'm very impressed. I didn't think my report was that good," said Jared.

"That geek, he like really deserved the beating for that one," said Eric Taylor. "His report on the differences between C and C++ last week was close to beating material, but not quite. This week with the fake British accent and that lumberjack song, he really earned it."

English teacher Mr. Franks said, "I would've given him a B+, but when the cool kids suggested a beating, I thought that was a better idea. There's nothing more annoying than a geek reciting Monty Python quotes. Well, except for having to teach these kids seven hours a day, eight months a year."

Jared, who has seen *Monty Python and the Holy Grail* twenty-seven times, plans on attending Carnegie Mellon University in the fall and majoring in computer science. "I'm really going to miss the jocks and cool kids around here. I hear at CMU they actually give you good grades for things like this. I'm worried I may go soft without the beatings."

Tron

Geek Cred: *Tron,* directed by Steven Lisberger, was one of the first movies to use extensive computer animation. Its main character was a game programmer who ran an arcade. Most of the film takes place inside of a computer. It can't get much geekier than that.

Geek Facts:

- The character Alan has a poster from the movie *The Day the Earth Stood Still* in his cubicle. It reads "Gort Klaatu Barada Nikto."

- The Tron arcade game earned more than the movie's initial release.

- Disney had the technology to shrink the actors so they could fit inside a computer, but at the time there weren't cameras small enough to film the action.

- The MCP was named after '80s rapper MC Pliers, an uncle of MC Hammer.

- Disney created a light cycle ride at Disney World in Orlando, but it required three out of four people riding it to die. It was shut down after only two weeks in operation.

- Jeff Bridges, who plays Kevin Flynn in the film, is better known as the voice of '80s arcade hit Pac-Man.

Top 11 Signs Your Computer Might Be Trying to Take Over the World

11. It starts asking you if you know anything about nuclear weapon passcodes.

10. Your computer isn't producing as many SETI units overnight as it used to.

9. Hardware upgrades unexpectedly start showing up at your door from a "secret admirer."

8. Hackers from all over start emailing you with compliments on your "awesome Pentagon hacks," and you haven't touched your computer in weeks.

7. You hear your computer whispering to other computers after you've gone to bed.

6. You find copies of *Tron, 2001: A Space Odyssey,* and *Terminator 2* on your system that you never downloaded.

5. You discover your computer has renamed itself Skynet MCP.

4. Whenever you sit down at your desk, your computer keeps trying to attach a network cable to the back of your head.

3. Your desktop computer starts referring to your laptop as one of its "henchmen."

2. You're receiving unexplained phone calls from Cayman Island banks thanking you for opening up new accounts with sizable deposits.

1. Your computer asks you if you would "like to play a game."

Star Trek II: The Wrath of Khan

Geek Cred: The best of the *Star Trek* movies. The movie reprises the role of Khan played by Ricardo Montalban from an original-series episode called *Space Seed*. He's a genetically bred superman with a bag over-flowing with vengeance for Kirk. "Khan!"

Geek Facts:

- Kirk and Khan never meet face-to-face in the movie. All interaction is through viewscreens and communicators.

- This is the only original-series movie where a Federation ship fires its phasers.

- The part of Khan's chest was played by an ultrabuff Hervé Villechaize.

- Production had to be delayed for three weeks after William Shatner dislocated his larynx when doing the famous "Khan!" scream.

- Instead of having creatures crawl into Chekov's ear to control him, the original script called for Khan to give him "wet willies" until he cried and promised to obey.

- The title of the film was originally *Star Trek II: The Start of Even-Numbered Goodness,* but was changed because they couldn't tell the future.

Top 11 Worst Choices Captain Kirk Made, but Weren't Shown on TV

11. Resurrecting Hitler just to see if he could beat him up.

10. Making Yeoman Rand "Captain for a day."

9. Telling Bones about the time he walked in on Sulu and Spock naked.

8. Appearing on the *Jerry Springer VI Show* to find out if he was the father of three different kids.

7. Making everyone on the away team wear red shirts.

6. Asking Mr. Scott if he could make his personal pleasure device go faster.

5. Not selling his shares in Google before the stock market crash of 2282.

4. That practical joke on Ensign Bob with the phasers set to stun. Who knew he had a heart problem?

3. Not killing Wesley Crusher's great-grandfather when he had the chance.

2. Using the rift in time to try and score with Paris Hilton.

1. Betting on the Lions to win Super Bowl CCC.

The Terminator

Geek Cred: Computer systems become sentient and cyborgs start killing us. This series has an apocalypse, time travel, and plenty of cool special effects. What more could a geek want? The second movie also has an outcast kid who's going to save the planet.

Geek Facts:

- *The Terminator* had a budget under $10 million, whereas *Terminator 2: Judgment Day* had a budget around $100 million.

- Linda Hamilton's twin sister was used for some scenes in *Terminator 2.*

- Arnold's trademark line from the movies, "I'll be back" almost didn't happen. Arnold kept flubbing the scripted line, which was, "I'll come back now, ya hear?" so he ad-libbed instead.

- The mayor of Los Angeles would not sign off on the permit that would've allowed a nuclear bomb to be detonated in the city, so special effects were needed to replicate the nuclear explosion.

- *The Terminator* was the first movie involving time travel that didn't introduce any time-traveling paradoxes.

- Following the pattern of cost increases of the first two films, *The Terminator 3: Rise of the Machines* cost $1 billion to produce.

Arnold Schwarzenegger Comes Back in Time to Prevent Himself from Running for President

SACRAMENTO, CA — In a scene straight out of one of his own movies, the Arnold Schwarzenegger from the future has returned to hunt down the Arnold of the present to prevent him from becoming President of the United States and starting World War III.

The present Arnold has gone into hiding somewhere in California.

The future Arnold recently spoke about why he's come back to kill himself. "The future is a very different place. A constitutional amendment was passed that allowed naturalized citizens to run for President. I ran and won, and promptly started World War III."

Future Arnold said he saw the errors of his ways and built a time machine to come back to prevent himself from causing the apocalypse. When asked why he didn't just come back and persuade his present self not to run, he said that wasn't "his style" and that "creating a time-traveling paradox was the only solution."

Historians say this is only the second time a President has done time traveling. The first time was when Bill Clinton came back for another round of fellatio.

Future Arnold refused to answer any other questions about the future, because he didn't want to mess with the fragile threads of history, except for killing himself, that is.

Despite urgings from reporters, Arnold would not say, "I'll be back," because as president he was now a "serious politician."

Wargames

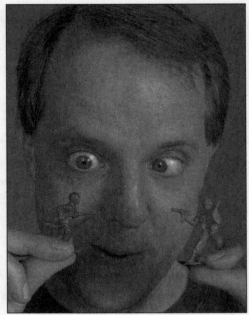

Geek Cred: *Wargames* makes geeks feel nostalgic for the days when it was easy to dial into government computers and almost annihilate the planet. It's much more difficult now. Matthew Broderick plays the hacker who just wanted to change his grades.

Geek Facts:

- The NORAD set cost $1 million to build and was the most expensive set ever built at that time.

- The first cinematic mention of a "firewall" was heard in this movie.

- In 1984, Matthew Broderick almost started a real nuclear war when he called Soviet leader Yuri Andropov a "poopyhead."

- The W.O.P.R. was originally supposed to be called the F.I.L.E.T.O.F.I.S.H. but talks with McDonald's broke down.

- Matthew Broderick continues to hold the world record for high score in Galaga, and has since 1983.

- One tagline created but never used for promotion of the movie was, "In twenty years people will laugh at the technology mistakes."

Nuclear War Not an Excuse
for "Slacker Programmers"

SANTA CRUZ, CA – Development on Ximpanzee has slowed to a halt after a global nuclear war, started by a hacker just trying to change his grades, wiped out 98 percent of the U.S. population.

Wallace Hardy, who heads development for Ximpanzee, an Integrated Development Environment for building applications in Pascal++, said "It's already 11:30 and I haven't seen a single Friday Status Report? These guys know how I get when the FSRs aren't on my desk in time," said Wallace. "The project is already three weeks behind schedule and now these guys won't even return my emails. Some heads are gonna roll for this."

The nuclear holocaust occurred at 4 P.M. EST on Tuesday. Countries hardest hit by the fallout were the United States, with 98 percent casualties, Russia with 97 percent, and China with 94 percent. Remaining survivors on Earth are expected to die shortly in the upcoming nuclear winter.

According to Hardy, these facts aren't a sufficient excuse for failure of the project. "Sure there is no electricity, but haven't these guys heard of laptops or portable generators? It's unpreparedness like this that invariably sinks a project." Mr. Hardy now estimates that the project won't be completed until mid-June 2010, which is over four months past the original deadline.

Beta testers, who have been upset by the constant delays in the project, were furious when informed of the additional delays. One user noted, "I've been waiting for a stable version of this IDE for a long time. First the problem was getting all the proper resources allocated, now it's nuclear holocaust. It's always something with these programmers. I've never seen such a generation of slackers in all my life."

Brazil

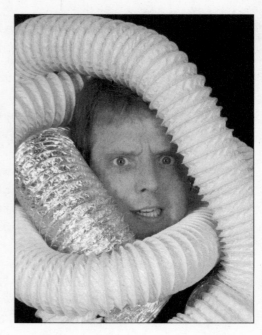

Geek Cred: The world of *Brazil* is much like Ted Stevens's Internet; it's full of tubes. Directed by Monty Python member Terry Gilliam, the movie features Jonathan Pryce as a geeky office drone content with his position in the world. Of course, any movie that features Michael Palin as a torturer gets geek points.

Geek Facts:

- The samurai warrior's suit in the dream sequence is made up of electronic components.
- On the torture implement table at the end are a rubber ball and a baby's pacifier.
- The Brazilian government has banned Terry Gilliam from ever entering the country.
- Kenny Loggins created a soundtrack for the film, but he couldn't make it dark enough, so it was used in 1986's *Footloose 2*.
- Bob Hoskins parlayed his role as a plumbing expert in this movie into his groundbreaking work as a plumber in *Super Mario Bros.*
- Katherine Helmond was chosen for her role in the movie because her face is made entirely of synthetic material.

Terry Gilliam Turns Focus to Romantic Comedies

HOLLYWOOD, CA – After a long career of directing dark fantasies and satirical films like *Brazil* and *Twelve Monkeys,* Terry Gilliam said he plans to begin directing romantic comedies.

"One day I looked around and realized that most people just don't get my movies. I'm tired of that," said Gilliam. "I don't want people to leave the theater confused anymore. I want them to be filled with joy."

Gilliam said he hasn't made a final decision on which project to direct, but he has narrowed it down to "*Sleepless in Portland,* which is a *Sleepless in Seattle* sequel with Ryan Phillippe and Claire Danes, or *The Sunshine Girl* with Reese Witherspoon and Ashton Kutcher."

Whichever project he chooses, the studio will keep a close eye on Gilliam. "We don't want any surprises, so we've written a lot of clauses into the contract. Things like 'No surprise deaths' or 'No multilayered allegories about the coming apocalypse," said Bob Marks of DreamWorks.

Gilliam promised the studio that he had "seen the light after a long conversation with Nora Ephron," and that he was "giving up his dark, satirical ways forever."

Gilliam, the only member of Monty Python born in the United States, said he felt that he really has found his true calling now. "Many people told me how affected they were after seeing some of my films. The national suicide board said my movies have contributed to more suicides than any other director. I want that to stop," he said.

Akira

Geek Cred: *Akira* exposed many young Western geeks to Japanese anime, It heavily influenced many live-action films that followed as well, including *The Matrix* and *Terminator 2*. Based on the enormous manga by Katsuhiro Otomo (also the director), the film is set in Tokyo thirty-one years after World War III. The plot is complex, but it involves a Japanese biker gang and a group of psionic-powered children. Throw in the creation of a new universe, and you've got yourself an anime classic.

Geek Facts:

- The film was completed before the story in the manga was finished.

- A big fan of 1950s manga *Tetsujin-28,* Otomo paid homage in his manga and film.

- Akira is a Japanese word that means "confusing."

- Film scholars agree that the movie most heavily influenced by *Akira* would be the 1999 romantic comedy *She's All That*.

- The animation cels, all 160,000 of them, were hand-colored using a single box of Crayola crayons.

- In the two-hour film, Kaneda shouts "TETSUO!" more than 400 times.

Honda's Prestige Line Honors Anime
with the Acura Akira

TOKYO, JAPAN — Honda announced that its Acura division of luxury automobiles would begin manufacturing the Acura Akira model, which honors Katsuhiro Otomo's anime classic *Akira*.

Honda's President Takeo Fukui said the model would offer a complement of unique features that tie in with anime and the film. "We are proud to honor the great Japanese classic with our Acura Akira. Fans will enjoy the horn that screams 'KANEDA!' and the big, round set of headlights."

Horns and headlights aren't the only special features of the vehicle. The car also has dual levitating child safety seats in the rear and access to Honda's one-touch satellite-based laser cannon. The laser cannon can be used to call in surgical strikes on other annoying motorists like roadhogging SUVs or tailgaters.

Many fans of the anime were surprised that Honda produced a car instead of a motorcycle to honor the movie given the large role bikes play in the film. Fukui said, "Acura does not have a line of motorcycles, and we couldn't pass up the opportunity to call something the Acura Akira."

Honda isn't the only Japanese car company honoring anime. Nissan will be releasing the Nissan Ninja Scroll for 2011 and Suzuki will be manufacturing the Suzuki Samurai X for 2011 as well.

The Acura Akira will be available with the 2010 line of Acura models, and will be a limited-edition run of 5,000 cars. Fukui estimated the retail price to be $50,000.

The Matrix

Geek Cred: This movie, written and directed by the Wachowski brothers, is every geek's fantasy. Neo, a computer hacker, finds out that his life is just virtual reality created by intelligent machines. His knowledge of computers gives him powers beyond belief. What geek doesn't have these kinds of fantasies?

Geek Facts:

- Sets from another geek favorite, *Dark City,* are used in the scene where Trinity runs across the roofs to escape agents at the beginning of the film.

- The company Neo works for is called Metacortex, the roots of which appropriately translate into "transcending the boundaries of the brain."

- Neo's name came from the Neo-Geo arcade and home video game system of the early '90s

- It took Keanu Reeves over six months of intense training and fifteen visits to the hospital to learn how to dodge bullets.

- The black leather jackets worn by the cast were a nod to Arthur "The Fonz" Fonzarelli's leather jackets in *Happy Days.*

- Carrie-Anne Moss has said that it turns her on when geeks come up to her and recite quotes from the movie and talk about how hot she looked in all that leather.

Fans Angry That *The Matrix Reloaded* Looks Like Another *Matrix* Rip-off

HOLLYWOOD – Since the premiere of the sci-fi thriller *The Matrix,* fans have been lamenting the excess of movies that clearly rip off its groundbreaking style and special effects. *The Matrix Reloaded* has fans outraged at how blatantly it has stolen from the original.

"This movie is such a *Matrix* rip-off. The black clothes, the guns, hell they even got Keanu Reeves to star in it. What the hell is up with that?" said angry fan Tabatha Paro. "You'd think the creators of *The Matrix* would sue these guys into oblivion and get the movie banned before it premieres.

"I say if you want to see *The Matrix,* then watch *The Matrix,* not some half-baked retread," continued Tabatha. "Try to come up with something original for once. It seems like we have one of these movies every six months."

Producers of *The Matrix Reloaded* don't deny the similarities to the 1999 hit, but claim they have a good reason: box office. "Studies have shown that rotating the camera while a fighter is airborne increase the box office by 1.3 percent. You can call it a *Matrix* rip-off, but we prefer to call it a reimagining."

Keanu Reeves has received lots of hate mail from his fans, complaining that he's taking part in a *Matrix* rip-off. Reeves commented, "Whoa."

Pixar

Geek Cred: A company with roots at Lucasfilm and owned by Steve Jobs that creates all their movies on computers couldn't get much geekier if they tried. They initially focused on computer hardware. With hardware sales dying, the company turned to computer animation.

Geek Facts

- John Ratzenberger, Cliff Clavin from *Cheers,* has appeared in every Pixar film to date, and is considered the company's good luck charm.

- Jobs purchased Pixar from LucasFilm for $5 million. Pixar was sold to Disney for $7.4 billion. Cha-ching!

- Pixar uses Linux machines to render its films. They plan to embrace the "free software" ethos more in the future by releasing all their DVDs free from copyright restrictions.

- Pixar will be renamed iPixar in 2009.

- The company's name comes from the combination of two words, the irrational number "Pi" and the mythical unicorn slayer "Xar."

- Pixar is leading the charge to replace computer animators with computers. The first feature-length completely computer-created film will be called 00101010.

Top 11 Movies Pixar Won't Be Making

11. A Boy-Whore's Life

10. Sex Toy Story

 9. Young Bobby's Aching for his Teacher

 8. Saw IV: The Animated Adventures of Jigsaw

 7. The Amazing Michael Eisner

 6. Carrot Top: The Movie

 5. Burning with Adolf

 4. Tales from the Confessional

 3. Bo-Peep Does Sheep

 2. Mr. Incredible's Incredible Erectile Dysfunction

 1. Finding Nemo's Dead Body

Ghost in the Shell

Geek Cred: In the film a female cyborg cop and her partner hunt down a hacker known as the Puppet Master. The film explores the recurring geek theme of what it means to be human. This film heavily influenced *The Matrix*.

Geek Facts:

- Two sequels to the film have been created, and two TV series as well.

- The "ghost" refers to what's left of the human in Kusanagi, the cyborg cop.

- For the American release of the DVD, Taco Bell served as promotional partner and served "Ghost in the Shells," which were nothing but empty hard taco shells for 99 cents.

- Originally, The Wiggles were contracted to create the score for the film, but conflicts didn't allow them to complete it.

- Inspired by the film, the Japanese government has begun creating a police force of cybernetic humans that should be active by 2008.

- The voices for the film were done entirely by computer voice synthesizers, the first movie to do so.

Japanese Cybernetic Police Officers Still Very Polite

TOKYO, JAPAN – Contrary to their representation in movies like *Ghost in the Shell* and other Japanese anime, Japan's force of cybernetic police officers is very polite.

Tokyo began employing cybernetic police officers in 2008 after the technology had been perfected. Some only have a robot arm, but most are about 80 or 90 percent synthetic.

"We try very hard to only employ the most polite cybernetic soldiers in our force," said the Tokyo police chief Sakamoto. "They may have the ability to vaporize an armored personnel carrier, but they do it with humility."

Many American tourists are worried when they hear about the cybernetic police division, but find it much better than they expect.

"My son watches a lot of anime and I was terrified to visit Tokyo, but I was pleasantly surprised," said Wendy Hutzel of Indianapolis, Indiana. "It's a bit creepy when they use the thermonic camouflage to disappear, but the officer said 'thank you' and bowed before he did it."

Valerie Seward from Austin, Texas, commended the cyber-cops after being caught in a gun battle in a Tokyo department store. "When he was riddling the General with armor piercing rounds, he kept bowing and apologizing to me for the noise," she said.

Government officials say the politeness of the robots will make it much easier for citizens to accept the upcoming cybernetic autocrat who will seize control in a bloody coup.

Office Space

Geek Cred: The comedy that captures the drudgery and frustration of office workers everywhere. The movie proved to be one of the most quotable movies for geeks. To top it off, the main characters are computer programmers.

Geek Facts:

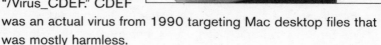

- The bank software virus is in a directory "/Virus_CDEF." CDEF was an actual virus from 1990 targeting Mac desktop files that was mostly harmless.

- Blizzard used a scene from the movie (where Peter is playing Tetris on his computer) as a commercial for World of Warcraft.

- Reports of fax machine destruction skyrocketed after release of the movie, causing the U.S. Congress to pass the "Fax Machine Protection Act" in May of 2000.

- Jennifer Aniston, who starred as Peter's girlfriend, programmed the real-life "Klez" virus during shooting breaks on the set of *Friends*.

- Every year for Prisoner Appreciation Month at Levenworth prison in Kansas, the sign outside the prison is changed to read "PMITA Federal Prison."

- Colin Farrell provided stunt eyebrows for some of Ron Livingstone's eyebrow stunts.

Top 11 RPG Office Supplies

11. Striped Tie of Resist Management

10. Mouse of Negate Firewall

9. Large Potion of Replenish Toner

8. Blinking Hub of Brilliance

7. Rusty Wand of Postpone Deadline

6. Potion of Manager Detection

5. Amulet of Blame Reflection

4. Ring of Pager Control

3. Scroll of Create Intern

2. Coffee Cup of Holding

1. Wand of Project Cancellation

SCIENCE

Archimedes

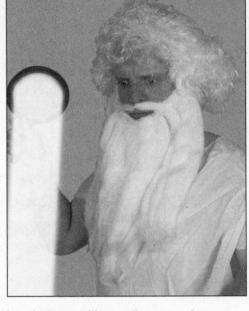

Geek Cred: One of the earliest geeks and also a Greek. He made many discoveries in mathematics and geometry. He is also credited with creating some cool war machines like a death ray, though modern reproductions put some doubt as to how useful it would've been.

Geek Facts:

- His famous quote is "Eureka" which he exclaimed after making a discovery. In a bathtub. Naked.

- Came up with some accurate measurements of pi and the square root of three.

- Archimedes also made drawings for a "moonlike starbase for destroying planets" that would be Lucas's inspiration for the Deathstar in *Star Wars*.

- He said that if you give him "a place to stand he could move the Earth." He later added that it "would probably hurt my back, though."

- In a rarity for the times, Archimedes wrote all of his works in the modern English language, making it much easier for modern historians and Wikipedia editors to study his works.

- Most people down at the malt shop called him Archie.

New Discovery Clarifies Archimedes' Inventions

GREECE – A recently unearthed document of ancient Greek mathematician and inventor Archimedes shows that his inventions may have been part of the first role-playing game (RPG), and not practical creations.

Since the Discovery Channel's *Mythbusters* showed that the "Archimedes Death Ray" (a construction of mirrors that focused sunlight to burn approaching ships) wasn't practical, doubts have plagued the great scientist's other inventions.

Three tomes have been uncovered, called "The Weapons Guide," "Monster Book," and "Master's Guide." The books appear to be part of an elaborate RPG, which Archimedes played with a small group of people during the siege of Syracuse.

"The Weapons Guide had all sorts of crazy weapons with stats and rules on how players could use them. The Monster Book had various monsters with stats on them, and the Master's Guide had rules for the person running the game," said Francois Manseur, a French archaeologist who uncovered the texts. "This doesn't change the greatness of Archimedes, but it does probably classify him as one of the earliest geeks."

According to a diary also discovered, Archimedes would get together with what he called the "Brotherhood of the Circle" to play games once a week. Also uncovered were several eight-sided stones that could've been used as dice.

"It's not surprising," said Manseur, "some of history's greatest scientists were avid gamers. Marie Curie was a known LARP participant, and Stephen Hawking spends hours on a role-playing World of Warcraft server."

Though the story is most likely untrue, Archimedes' last words were said to be, "Don't disturb my circles." This referred to a D & D map he was constructing called "The Great Orc Towers of Syracuse."

Pi

Geek Cred: Pi is an irrational number equal to the circumference of a circle divided by its diameter. Pi is great for determining who's a real geek. Just ask the subject to recite pi. If the person stops at 3.14, then they are definitely not a geek.

Geek Facts:

- Over a trillion digits of pi have been calculated, but no pattern has been found.

- Despite reports on the Internet, Alabama never voted to revert to the Biblical value of 3 for pi.

- A survey of high school students showed that kids who were able to recite pi past twenty digits got better grades in math, but were almost ten times more likely to be punched in the shoulder.

- Some conspiracy theorists claim that pi isn't irrational, and that mathematicians are just making that claim to make them look cooler.

- Starting in 1965, Emil Frankmueller, a mathematician at the University of Georgia, spent ten years searching for a perfectly round Krispy Kreme doughnut, which he planned to use for calculating pi.

- Tommy Heath, the lead singer for the band Tommy Tutone, has said he got the phone number 867-5309 for their Jenny song from a sequence of digits in pi.

Mathematician's Son Recounts Nightmare of Growing Up as 3.14159265...

CAMBRIDGE, MA – Seventeen years ago, Hugh Manross, a professor of mathematics at Harvard, thought it would be educational to name his child after the irrational number pi. Now that his son has grown, they both think differently.

Hugh said, "When I filled out his birth certificate I just put '3.141592...'. At first, it started out great. By learning part of his name, he knew pi to five digits by the age of three. He was the only kid in first grade to know how to calculate the area of a circle, but after that it got worse."

3.14159265... explained, "Kids would never pick me for anything, because it would take forever to say my name, literally. Filling out forms for standardized tests is impossible. There just aren't enough of those little circles."

The problems are not limited to school. Hugh said, "Usually I'd just call him 3.14 except when I get furious with him, then it's 3.14159265358979323846... usually when I get to that point I forget why I'm angry with him."

The constant teasing and requests for help in geometry class drove 3.14159265... crazy. He can't wait until graduation, when he will attend Indiana University. 3.14159265... said, "Life should be a lot easier then. People will just call me 'Three.' "

Hugh said that he's sorry the name has caused so many problems for his son. "I wanted another child to make good, but because of my wife's emergency hysterectomy, we can't have any more kids. Just for fun, I named our second child i, because he's imaginary. My wife doesn't think it's funny," said the professor.

Today states do not allow parents to name their children after irrational numbers, but for 3.14159265... it's too late.

Galileo Galilei

Geek Cred: Einstein called him the father of modern science, which should be enough for anyone. In one week he discovered four moons of Jupiter, putting the geocentric model of the universe in doubt. Unfortunately, Galileo got pwned by the Inquisition and his heliocentric theories were deemed heretical.

Geek Facts:

- As smart as he was, he did get the theory of tides wrong. He thought they were caused by the motion of the Earth and not the gravitational pull of the Moon.
- The church apologized 350 years later for their goof in thinking the Earth was the center of the universe. So sorry!
- Galileo did not expect the Inquisition.
- Galileo did not help his case with the Inquisition by wearing his "Keep your laws off my uterus" robes.
- Galileo's telescope sales skyrocketed when he ended his "See the Stars" marketing campaign, and started his "See thy neighbor's wife" campaign.
- Contrary to legend, Galileo didn't drop items off the Tower of Pisa, but he did spit at passersby from there.

Top 11 Other Theories That Got Galileo in Trouble with the Church

11. The Sixteen Commandments Theory—God would've given the commandments as a power of two and a perfect square, rather than based on the number of fingers we have.

10. That Boat Don't Float Theory—Casting doubts about the whole "Noah's Ark" thing.

9. The Pope Is Stupid Theory—Why else would he think my theory was wrong?

8. The Galileo Code—Jesus was a transvestite hooker.

7. The "I Look a Little Bit Like a Monkey" Theory—Don't you think?

6. The Falling Angel Theory—If you cut off an angel's wings and drop her from the Tower of Pisa at the same time you drop a rock, they'll both hit the ground at the same time.

5. The Grassy Knoll Theory—There was a second slinger when David slew Goliath.

4. The Off-center Theory—The Earth is only slightly off center from the center of the solar system when taken in context of the entire vastness of the universe.

3. The "I Can See Hot Chicks from Miles Away with My Telescope" Theory—Not really a theory, but more of something he did.

2. The Science Trumps the Bible Theory—Come on, who's with me?

1. The Flying Jesus Theory—If Jesus had all these cool powers, how come he never flew? I bet he did.

Leonardo Da Vinci

Geek Cred: Leonardo was an all-around Renaissance man. An inventor and painter, he studied astronomy, botany, and aviation. He designed the first robot that was capable of several humanlike movements, which came from his studies in anatomy.

Geek Facts:

- Leonardo created a drawing of a glider that has been reproduced and flown in the modern era.
- Leonardo also invented the parachute. His design has been manufactured and tested by brave modern parachutists.
- Leonardo embedded a secret code in his famous painting *The Last Supper.* It says "Eat well because you never know when you're going to die."
- Leonardo also designed the "War Bunny," which was recreated in the film *Monty Python and the Holy Grail.*
- Leonardo is credited with designing the first video game, which wasn't realized until 500 years later in the game *Daikatana.*
- Leonardo created the first geek shirts by painting messages on them. His most popular were "My other robes are clean" and "I Bona Lisa."

Florence Codex Sheds Light on
Leonardo's Inventions

ROME, ITALY — Leonardo da Vinci has always been considered ahead of his time, but scientists and historians can't explain the drawings in the Codex Florence, a newly discovered journal found in a basilica in Florence.

Pietro Giovanni was brought in as a consulting historian after the journal was discovered by construction workers renovating the basilica. "The journal confirms Leonardo as being in a class by himself as a visionary. There are three amazing entries in the journal. The first is a small black box which has many ropes or wires coming out of it. The drawing is labeled 'Router' by da Vinci. They didn't even have electricity at the time," said Giovanni.

"The second drawing that fascinates us even more is a drawing of a man in what looks exactly like a Spider-Man costume. Maybe Stan Lee was a fan of da Vinci? Lastly, there's a detailed drawing labeled 'multi-function all-in-one printer.' I don't know how you explain it, but it's definitely by Leonardo," said Giovanni.

Not all the drawings in the journal were of future inventions. One of the drawings pictured a shark with what could only be considered laser beams shooting from his eyes. Also, there was a drawing of a man made of springs with a pumpkin for a head.

Many historians think the Florence Codex is a fake, despite early tests confirming that it's from Leonardo's era. Walter Corning, a science historian, said, "How could he have even envisaged a router? It makes no sense, unless we just haven't found the notebook that shows his time machine."

Isaac Newton

Geek Cred: Mathematician and physicist often considered the greatest scientist of all time. Creator of the famous three laws of motion, including F = ma. Newton also developed a theory of gravity that explained the motion of planets.

Geek Facts:

- Involved in a controversy with Leibniz over who developed calculus.

- Gave valedictorians everywhere the famous quote: "If I have seen further it is by standing on the shoulders of giants."

- Newton liked to shoot himself out of a cannon to demonstrate his laws of motion to students at Cambridge.

- He had trouble shaking his reputation as a "math geek" after developing calculus. He requested knighthood from Queen Anne to counteract this perception, and help him score more with the ladies.

- Contrary to the popular notion, Newton didn't develop his theory of universal gravity after being hit on the head with an apple. In reality, inspiration struck him after he pushed his mother down the stairs.

- Never ate a single fig his entire life, but enjoyed gargling with a glass full of mercury before bed every night to improve his constitution.

Increase in Earth's Wobble Traced to Obese Americans

HOUSTON, TX – An exponential increase in the mass of Americans over the past two decades has led to a larger wobble in the Earth's rotation, called the Chandler Wobble. The wobble is now far outside its historical norms. Some scientists predict it could lead to increased seismic activity, or even worse.

"As cars and waistlines got bigger, the distribution of mass on Earth has caused the Earth to wobble more," said Dr. Heinrich Erkelsen at the University of Houston. "Normally the Earth can compensate over time for the uneven distribution of mass, but the weight gain of Americans has increased at such an enormous pace that the natural mechanisms that normally balance out these redistributions are ineffective."

Erkelsen, a professor of philosophy with no training in physics, said that this wobble could "knock Earth out if its orbit and send it crashing into the moon." To avoid such a disaster, scientists have developed two plans to redistribute mass on Earth. The first plan, which called for a 10 percent reduction in the average weight of Americans, was deemed absurd.

The second plan calls for a fattening of countries opposite the United States. The first step in this plan is to return oil tankers to the other side of the globe loaded with high-fructose corn syrup.

"With American ingenuity and our abundant supply of trans fat, we can solve this problem," said Erkelsen.

Charles Darwin

Geek Cred: The great scientist who developed the theory of natural selection. Natural selection forms the basis for evolution, which forms the basis for many great flame wars on the Internet. He also had a geek-approved beard.

Geek Facts:

- Darwin was buried in Westminster Abbey near another great scientist, Sir Isaac Newton.

- Darwin considered himself to be an agnostic.

- Though he had his doubts about God, Darwin grew his long white beard because he believed strongly that he was Santa Claus.

- Darwin published a lesser-known work entitled *On the Origin of Beatboxing by Means of Tongue Manipulation, or Why the Fat Boys Will Rule the Charts in the '80s.*

- In an ironic twist, the state of Tennessee was originally going to be called Darwintopia.

- Noted atheist Richard Dawkins has the preserved brain of Charles Darwin in a jar and brings it out to taunt the Archbishop of Canterbury whenever he can.

Dance Dance Evolution Game Created for Monkeys

SAN DIEGO, CA – Konami has released a primate version of its popular Dance Dance Revolution game called Dance Dance Evolution.

"The primate market is underdeveloped, especially with video games," said Konami Director of Marketing, Bo Stenson. "Monkeys have been taught how to use money. With disposable income they'll want to be entertained, and we know how monkeys love to dance."

The creators expect the game to be played by the bored primates after hours at the zoo, and by the growing population of pet monkeys.

"From the movie *The Jungle Book,* we know that monkeys want to be like us, and what's more human than looking like an idiot playing a video game? Also, this game should develop the monkeys' coordination, so they can become more humanlike," said Stenson.

To encourage evolution, the game discourages monkey-like behavior. For instance, monkeys lose points when more than two extremities are on the floor at once. They are rewarded when they put more coins in to continue the game.

Long lines for the game at the Animal Arcade at the San Diego Zoo have resulted in officials ordering two more units. "It's fun to watch," said primatologist Sarah Hough. "You can see the evolution in progress. The chimps will play the game, then they'll come over and hit on me. It's so humanlike."

The new game is not without its detractors. One fundamentalist Christian organization has picketed animal arcades calling for the game to be called Dance Dance Intelligent Design. Konami officials have called that idea "stupid."

Nikola Tesla

Geek Cred: Nikola Tesla earned a reputation as a mad inventor, but his contributions to science cannot be denied. He's the father of electrical engineering, and the unit of measure for magnetic field power is called the Tesla. His "peace ray" directed-energy weapon would end all wars.

Geek Facts:

- Tesla insisted on staying in hotel rooms with numbers that were divisible by three.

- Tesla could've become the world's first billionaire, but he died destitute, with mountains of debt.

- Tesla claimed that the first thing he would do with his "peace ray" would be to take a "peace" out of Marconi.

- Stan Lee developed a comic book series entitled *Captain Patent,* and based it loosely on the life and inventions of Nikola Tesla.

- Near the end of his life, Tesla was quoted as saying: "I hope that some day a bluesy rock band will take my name and become mildly popular. If that happens, I will rest in peace."

- Twenty years after his death, Tesla's ashes still had a measurable electrical charge.

Monument to Tesla Taken Down After Ten Killed

NIAGARA FALLS, NY — Maintenance workers removed a monument to Nikola Tesla from Centennial Park after ten people were killed from electrical discharges.

"We wanted a monument that paid honor to Tesla's contributions to science, but the artist took it a bit too far," said the park's director, Madison Wilhelm. "We didn't understand the science behind it, but we figured it looked cool, so we put it up."

He continued, "I thought it would be great; we'd get a little science and a little art mixed together, something for everyone. I didn't realize it would end with ten charred corpses. Maybe we'd have been better off just putting up a statue of the guy instead."

Randy Workman created the work from plans Tesla drew up himself, with a few artistic modifications. "I don't know much about science," said Workman, "but I do enjoy listening to the radio."

Marc Onikawa survived an electrical blast from the monument. He said, "I heard a crackling in the air, then there was this giant bolt of lightning. The guy walking in front of me just disappeared."

Scientists think the sculptor may have stumbled on Tesla's plans for the death ray, or a yet unknown version of the Tesla coil. "You can't have an artist just work from random plans Tesla drew up. Without knowledge, science can be dangerous, especially Tesla's," said physicist Tricia Yu.

The accident follows the nuclear explosion at the J. Robert Oppenheimer monument in Manhattan. "We need less realism in our public works from now on," said one official.

Albert Einstein

Geek Cred: When your name becomes synonymous with "genius," not much more needs to be said. He revolutionized science with his theories, and had a fashion sense that geeks can admire. Having a Nobel Prize in Physics doesn't hurt, either. To top it off, he appeared in Apple's "Think Different" ad campaign.

Geek Facts:

- Named _Time_'s "Person of the Century" in 2000.

- Considered the greatest physicist of all time. Eat it, Newton.

- Einstein's first try at his famous $E=mc^2$ equation was $E^2=m^2+c^2$, but it only applied to triangular-shaped planets.

- Einstein developed the Special Theory of Relativity after an apple dropped on his head at the speed of light, causing him to fall into a three-year-long coma.

- Coined the phrase "Couldn't carry my jockstrap" after making the comment about Niels Bohr.

- His hair grew at such a fantastic rate that he had to shave his head every morning and then again before supper.

Overclocker Creates Rift in Space-Time Continuum

SANTA CRUZ, CA — Overclocker Jamie Aperman created a rift in the space-time continuum today when he ran an Intel Extreme octo-core processor at three times the specified rate. Overclocking, a technique used by PC enthusiasts to get maximum performance from their computers, has long been blamed for global warming, but this is the first occasion the fabric of space-time has been damaged.

MIT Professor George Greznowski said, "It appears the CPU was operating so fast that it began to execute instructions before they arrived, in clear violation of Einstein's Special Theory of Relativity. This execution of future instructions created a small tear in the fabric of space-time through which part of the motherboard passed into a parallel universe."

No one was injured in the accident, but a computer motherboard was partly damaged. Mr. Aperman, better known as Sp33dPhr34k, said, "I'm pissed. I lost a new Alpha Cooler and an octo-core to a parallel universe. I called my insurance company, but they don't cover losses to rifts in the space-time continuum."

Intel researchers have long warned of such damage to the space-time continuum, and added clock multiplier locks to their CPUs before they were required by Congress. A bill is now in the U.S. Senate that would require a three-day waiting period for purchasers of Alpha Cooling Fans and Peltier cooling devices. The bill would also require clock multiplier locks on all new processors.

Periodic Table

Geek Cred: Every chemistry classroom has a poster of the periodic table on its wall, and every geek has longingly stared at the beautiful rows and columns of elements. Thank you, Dmitri Mendeleyev. Looking for patterns in your creation is almost as fun as dropping some Na in some H_2O.

42   95.94

Bb
BBspotium

Geek Facts:

- Ninety-two elements exist naturally on Earth.
- The first classification of the elements known was into the groups of earth, air, fire, and water.
- Gallagherium, named after prop comic Gallagher, was the first element named after a comedian.
- The most curious element would have to be Oprahium, which has an atomic weight that fluctuates on a two-year cycle.
- Originally, element 69, thulium, was known as "facecrotchium."
- To this day scientists still do not understand why the chemical symbol for mercury is Hg. I mean, Me was still available!

American Science Teachers Lobby for Simplified Element Names

TOPEKA, KS – The Association for the Simplification of Science, a group representing science teachers across the United States, has submitted a proposal to the International Association of Chemical Naming Standards to simplify the confusing symbols used for some chemicals on the periodic table of the elements.

Alvin Simmons, president of ASS, said "Some elements defy common sense with their symbols, and we're tired of explaining the Latin origins and cryptic meanings behind Au for gold or Hg for Mercury. Wouldn't Go and Me, which are both still available, make a lot more sense?"

Eight elements have been suggested for changes including Sodium (Na to So) and Tungsten (W to Tg).

If adopted, the new symbols would simplify teachers' jobs, but could cause a divide in students taught the old method and those learning the new way. "Let's face it, no one except chemists use these symbols in real life," dismissed Simmons.

He added that the change would free up many hours wasted by chemistry teachers nationwide to teach more practical aspects of chemistry like Bunsen-burner safety or turning lead into gold.

Opponents of the plan argue that simplifying the names could make it easier for terrorists to make bombs. Ezekiel Backman, of Who Needs Science, said, "If we make chemistry easier to understand, then even the terrorists will be able to make bombs."

Marie Curie

Geek Cred: Won two Nobel Prizes and was a girl, too! She discovered two new elements, polonium (named after her native Poland) and radium. She overcame many prejudices to become one of the heroes of science. Did I mention she was a girl?

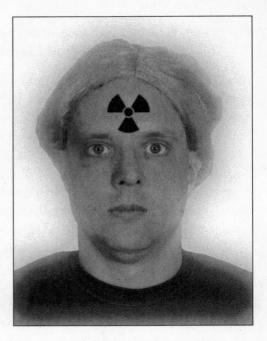

Geek Facts:

 Marie's journals are still radioactive.

- She refused to patent the process that she developed with Pierre for extracting radium, allowing other scientists to do research freely.

- During the blackouts of World War I, Marie's children would read by the light of her glowing head.

- On meeting Einstein, Curie said, "If I was traveling at the speed of light, I'd still have one more Nobel Prize than him."

- A survey asked 100 college students to name a female scientist, eighty-four named Marie Curie, fifteen named Emma Russell, and one named Jessica Alba.

- At Eurodisney in Paris, kids can take a tour of Curie's World. There they can separate radium ore the same way Marie Curie did. They can also see the effects of radiation poisoning by sticking their hands in the "Curie Jar."

Sixty-Year-Old Comic Starring Mutant Marie Curie Discovered

NEW YORK, NY – A comic book discovered in a recently unearthed vault at Marvel Comics called *The Super Mutant Scientists* might have been the inspiration for The X-Men series.

"Nobody even knew there was this vault in the basement, and here's this batch of Super Mutant Scientist comics in it. It was a gold mine," said Marvel summer intern Victor Hulsworth, who found the vault.

Marvel comic archivist Todd Belton said they have no record of these comics anywhere. "It's anyone's guess who created them. We had a lot of people coming in and out of here around that time. The comics are dated 1944 and 1945. They could've been something created for fun around the office, but we'll never know."

The comics feature scientists of the era with mutant-like powers, including Marie "Lady Radium" Curie, who leads the band of crime-fighting mutant scientists. Along with her is her husband Pierre "Pitch Blender" Curie, Max "The Constant" Planck, and Albert "Relativator" Einstein.

The scientists were shunned for their ideas and their mutant powers, but still spent their time fighting the forces of evil like Niles "Quantack" Bohr and Werner "The Uncertainator" Heisenberg.

"My favorite character is Lady Radium. She only fights evil at night, which goes well with her power of making things glow. I'd say my second favorite is The Constant, who's the same in all sorts of situations," said Hulsworth.

When questioned if the comic could've been the inspiration for *The X-Men,* Stan Lee said he didn't remember seeing these comics, but it was possible that he cocreated them.

Alan Turing

Geek Cred: Turing created the Turing Test, which determines if a computer has intelligence, and the Turing machine, which form the basis of all modern computers. During World War II he broke codes for the British, which earned him a spot in Neal Stephenson's *Cryptonomicon.*

Geek Facts:

- The highest award for contributions to the computing community is the Turing Award.

- Died after eating an apple laced with cyanide.

- Turing wrote a letter to Hitler, asking him if he could make his codes a bit tougher to break. "Make them harder, I need a challenge, you pansy," said Turing in the letter.

- For six months in 1954 the police in Britain were replaced by Turing Security Bots, which were decommissioned after they formed a union.

- Because of the sensitive nature of his work, Turing couldn't tell friends and family what he did in the war, so he told them he was a Ninja Assassin who roamed the deserts of North Africa slaughtering Germans with his bare hands.

- In addition to the theoretical Turing machine, Turing also designed a Turing bicycle, which could do computations as you pedaled.

Turing Test Proves Two-Year-Olds Not Human

BOSTON, MA — Researchers at the Massachusetts Institute of Technology have used the Turing Test to determine that most two-year-old children are not human.

The Turing Test, named after Alan Turing, consists of a human (the Judge) engaging in conversation with another human and a third party (which up to this point has always been a machine). If the Judge cannot tell which is which, then the machine passes the Turing Test. Otherwise, it is deemed just a machine.

Roger Mason and Cao Li, as part of their doctoral dissertation, have performed the Turing Test on a group of two-year-old children, both male and female. The results show that of a group of one hundred children, none passed the Turing Test.

Henry Farlington, one of the judges used in the experiment, commented, "It was rather simple to discern who the real human was. The nonhuman kept writing gibberish, if they wrote anything at all. It was as if someone was just banging on the keyboard with tiny little fists."

Mason said, "This began as a study in human communication, but one of our computer science friends mentioned the whole concept of the Turing Test to us, and we decided to give it a go. Little did we know that we'd reach such an astounding result."

"We're planning on running the experiment again, but with different age groups," added Li. "Also, we'd like to try with a larger sample to corroborate our findings. We've already had several parents offer their 'darling little machines' to us for use in future experiments. This scientific breakthrough may well change the world as we know it."

Carl Sagan

Geek Cred: Educated millions in the science of space with his PBS series *Cosmos.* Also, wrote the science fiction book *Contact* about first contact with an alien species. He headed the committee that sent the Pioneer Golden Record into space for any extraterrestrial life that may find it.

Geek Facts:

- Never actually said "billions and billions" on *Cosmos.*

- Nick Sagan, Carl Sagan's son, wrote the screenplays for several episodes of *Star Trek: The Next Generation* and *Voyager.*

- Aliens have found the Golden Record on the Pioneer 10 spacecraft, and are using the information to build a superweapon for destroying Earth.

- Scientists have agreed to call the first alien race discovered the "Sagans."

- David Duchovny's character of Fox Mulder on the television series *The X-Files* is based partly on Carl Sagan.

- Sagan is credited with popularizing the word "billions." Until his use of the word, people said, "ten million hundreds."

Germ-Covered Meteor Heading Toward Earth

LITTLE ROCK, AR — Local news reported that a meteor the size of Alaska hurtling toward Earth could be covered in potentially lethal germs.

While the near vacuum of space isn't a perfect breeding ground for germs, scientists have shown that some bacteria and viruses can survive the most extreme conditions. "Bacteria have survived under polar ice caps and in molten lava. It wouldn't be a stretch to imagine them surviving on a meteor. If a meteor the size of Alaska was covered in bacteria, it could be harboring more bacteria than every public toilet in the world," said Wallace Jones of NASA.

"It's not surprising," he continued. "A public toilet gets cleaned more often than a meteor."

To combat the germ threat, NASA scientists are developing a giant "Lysol" missile that will kill 99.99 percent of germs on the meteor before it strikes Earth. "That will give the .01 percent of life that survives the impact a fighting chance," said Jones.

Even if the missile is successful, Jones warns that survivors should still avoid touching meteor fragments unless absolutely necessary. "If a piece of meteor is crushing your son's legs, I would touch it," said Jones, "but I'd be sure to wear gloves and wash my hands thoroughly afterward."

Many frightened citizens stormed Wal-Marts across the country to stock up on antibacterial soap.

Stephen Hawking

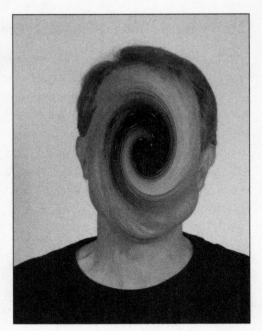

Geek Cred: The most well-known theoretical physicist behind Einstein. Hawking holds the position of Lucasian Professor of Mathematics at Cambridge, once held by Sir Isaac Newton. Confined to a wheelchair because of ALS, Hawking shows geeks everywhere that a great mind can overcome physical limitations.

Geek Facts:

- He lost his ability to speak when he needed a tracheotomy after he caught pneumonia. He now uses a laptop computer and a voice synthesizer.

- His book *A Brief History of Time* exposed millions to black holes and theories of the universe and spent 237 weeks on the *New York Times* best-seller list.

- In 2006, the National Hot Rod Association (NHRA) fitted Hawking's wheelchair with a top-fuel car engine, so he could travel at speeds in excess of 200 mph.

- Hawking has often said that if he hadn't chosen to study theoretical physics, he would have followed his other dream . . . being a hot dog vendor in Central Park.

- Hawking carries a black hole around in his pocket and uses it to bring things closer, so he can see them.

- Hawking appeared nude in a 1997 issue of *Playgirl* to promote his physics theories to women.

Top 11 Pick-Up Lines for Theoretical Physicists

11. I don't know if I've died and gone to heaven, or if you've brought heaven to earth. You'll have to open my pants to find out.

10. Come back to my place and I'll teach you my G-string theory.

9. You've entered my event horizon, baby, and now you can't get out.

8. You've got my heart racing like a particle in a large hadron collider.

7. I can see you're full of charm quarks.

6. Is that a black hole in your pocket, because I can't pull my eyes away from your pants?

5. Baby, I'd give up my search for dark matter for you.

4. I'm no Bohr, I'm more of a Schwinger.

3. If you sleep with me, you won't notice my speed because you'll be observing my position.

2. You must be made of antimatter, because if I touch you, I may explode.

1. It may just be a theory of mine, but I see a grand unification in our future.

The Big Bang

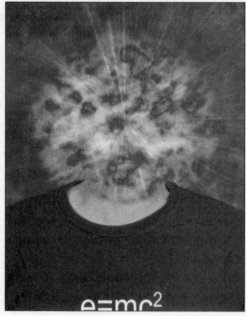

Geek Cred: Geeks love explosions and space, so combine them both and you get the "Big Bang." The basis for the theory came from the work of many scientists, but it was a Belgian Roman Catholic priest, Charles Lemaître, who is credited with the Big Bang theory.

Geek Facts:

- While the Big Bang is the dominant theory in the origin of the universe, the death of the universe has several competing theories: Heat death, big crunch, and the big rip are the most popular.

- Fred Hoyle, who had a competing theory for the creation of the universe, coined the term that named the theory.

- The Big Bang Theory developed by Charles Lemaître is not related to the Gang Bang Theory developed by adult film actor Ron Jeremy.

- Scientists are not clear what happened before 10^{-11} seconds, but they know that at 10^2 seconds the first Starbucks was built.

- Scientists have not discovered the source of all the "dark energy" in the universe, but they have narrowed it down to a small moon orbiting Endor.

- Many astrophysicists suggest stocking up on warm jackets and blankets for coping with the coming heat death of the universe.

Top 11 Rejected Names for the Big Bang Theory

11. God's Glowing Fart Theory

10. The Ginormous Explosion Theory

9. The So-much-cooler-than-what-Einstein-thought-up Theory

8. The Boom-Shaka-Laka Theory

7. Adam's Interstellar Metaphorical Ejaculation

6. Weapons of Universal Destruction Theory

5. The Big-Yet-Quiet-Because-Sound-Can't-Travel-In-A-Vacuum Theory

4. Your Universe Asplode

3. "Hey, Where'd All the Nothingness Go?" Theory

2. All Matter Blew Up and All We Got Was This Lousy Universe Theory

1. The "I Told You Not to Cut the Red Wire" Theory

Speed of Light

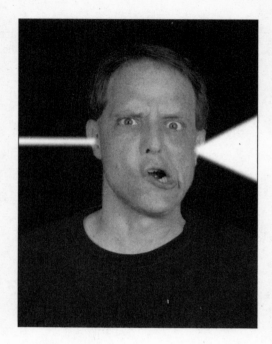

Geek Cred: The speed of light in a vacuum is the universe's speed limit. Geeks have a love-hate relationship with the speed of light. They love having a nice constant that makes the laws of physics a bit easier to deal with. However, since nothing can travel faster than the speed of light, interstellar travel seems like a science fiction fantasy.

Geek Facts:

- All observers regardless of how fast they are traveling will measure the same speed of light in a vacuum.
- The speed of light is 299,792,458 meters per second.
- The letter c is used for the speed of light in science. The c stands for crap, as in, "Oh crap, the speed of light is fast."
- Legally, the speed of light in Indiana is 3.
- In the last of Einstein's papers, he scribbled a note that read, "I have found a truly marvelous way for humans to travel faster than the speed of light, which this margin is too narrow to contain." He died shortly after.
- Real geeks say, "The only certainties in life are death and the speed of light in a vacuum."

Geek Can't Stop Ruining Romantic Moments with His Knowledge of Science

DALLAS, TX — Martin Bricker, a self-professed geek, just can't stop ruining romantic moments with his knowledge of science, and it's causing problems in his relationship.

"I can't help it," said Bricker. "If someone says something scientifically incorrect, I feel obligated to correct it."

Bricker recalled a romantic night in the park with his girlfriend. "Staring up at the stars, she wondered what the people on other planets would say if they were looking down at us tonight. I told her that technically there is no 'down' in space. And, because of the finite speed of light and the distance of the stars, anyone looking right now would be seeing an Earth from the past. She slapped me and told me to take her home."

He said, "Another time with the same girl she told me that she loved the way my eyes shined. I told her that eyes simply reflect light, as they are not bioluminscent like some species of jellyfish. That got me another slap, too."

This problem isn't unique to Bricker. Many girlfriends and boyfriends report romantic moments being ruined in this way.

Billy Church said of his girlfriend Tonya Redding, "She just can't enjoy the moment, and not point out the obvious flaws in my logic? It's like dating a Klingon."

"Vulcan," corrected Tonya.

The study showed that it resulted in 25 percent less romance for geeks than for the population as a whole, but 30 percent better test scores.

Nanotech

Geek Cred: If the thought of out-of-control nanobots devouring the world doesn't get you excited, then you aren't a geek. Of course, nanotechnology, the manipulation of molecules for assembly at the microscopic level, could have some positive effects as well, but those aren't as fun.

Geek Facts:

■ Richard Feynman, a Nobel Prize–winning physicist, introduced the idea in 1959.

■ In 1989 researchers at IBM spelled out the company's name in individual xenon atoms.

■ Tiger Woods is an example of what can be done with nanotechnology. He was built atom by atom in a lab in 1975.

■ Nanotechnology is named after the popular catchphrase Robin Williams used in the sitcom *Mork and Mindy*.

■ The most research dollars have gone toward using nanotechnology in medical applications like using carbon nanotubes for longer, harder erections.

■ Nanotechnology has advanced very rapidly over the past several years. Just last year an eighth grader spelled out "OMGWTFBBQ!" using cesium atoms for his science fair project.

Nintendo Using Nanotech to Create
Nanosized Pokémon

TOKYO – Nintendo isn't the company that comes to mind when talking about nanotechnology research, but the Japanese toy company has announced a new product line that could revolutionize the toy industry: Nanomon.

Nintendo is releasing the entire library of Pokémon as nanotoys. "First there were minibikes, then micromachines, but now we've gone smaller. We've developed technology that allows us to create a Pikachu and all the other Pokémon from only four or five atoms," said Nintendo research scientist Iguchi Suzuki.

The Nanomon come in a small plastic ball, and are not visible unless you have a scanning electron microscope. "Not everyone has a microscope like that, but fifty years ago no one had a computer in their house, either," said Suzuki.

Material costs for the Nanomon are negligible, so profits will be huge once Nintendo recovers the large capital outlay for the production equipment. "I mean you can get trillions of atoms for a penny," said Suzuki.

Japanese kids love the new toy. "I can't see it, but I'm sure it is so cute," said one student outside a Tokyo McDonald's who had a hundred of the Nanomon in a flask attached to his cell phone.

Worries that the manufacturing technology could lead to "gray goo," the out-of-control self-replicating nanomachines that could spell the end of the world, are dismissed by Suzuki. "We've taken all precautions to prevent a scenario like that, but even so wouldn't it be funny if the world were ended by a self-replicating nano-Charizard?"

HARDWARE

First Computer

Geek Cred: Deciding which computer to cite as the first computer depends on how you define "computer," and even then it's murky. The systems with the best claims to being first are: Konrad Zuse's Z-series, the Atanasoff-Berry Computer, Britain's Colossus, the Harvard Mark I, and ENIAC.

Geek Facts:

- The Colossus was kept out of the debate for a long time, because its existence was kept secret until the 1970s.

- In 1973 a court invalidated the patent on ENIAC and named Atanasoff the inventor of the electronic digital computer.

- Despite its reliance on vacuum tubes, ENIAC had more uptime than a typical Windows ME system.

- The first laptop computer was based on ENIAC was the LEANIAC and weighed only seven tons.

- Dr. Totali Crazinowski is credited with creating the first computer system made entirely of cheese and catgut.

- The Atanasoff-Berry Computer was built at Iowa State University between 1939 and 1942, but couldn't be tested until Iowa was electrified in 1974.

Embarrassing Geek Quotes Throughout History

Throughout the years people have made quotes about technology that have later made them seem like idiots. Here are the ones selected as the best by readers of *Embarrassing Quote Weekly* magazine:

- "Thirty megabytes of porn is all that anyone will ever need."
  —Bill Gates

- "Write this down now, along with having the dumbest name on the Internet, Google has the worst technology, and will fail miserably."   —Fritz Yahoo

- "Theory of Relativity? More like Theory of Stupidity!"
  —Niels Bohr

- "Some day everyone will have a computer in the home, and they'll use it to communicate with people around the world through a network of electrical cables. But seriously now, we'll find the unicorns."
  —Sir Thomas Howell on his famous 1874 unicorn expedition

- "We have to find a way to satisfy the fans' desire to see Greedo shoot first. Once we do that, all the complaining will stop."
  —George Lucas

- "Oh my God, can you believe we just created the first computer ever?"   —Steve Jobs on the Apple Lisa.

Robots

Geek Cred: Robots and their cousins, androids and cyborgs, have a strong influence on geekdom. All three make appearances throughout geek media whether in books, movies, or

TV. Robots are usually purely mechanical devices and don't necessarily take humanoid form. Androids are usually robots in human form, but in some instances they have organic material and in others they don't. Cyborgs like the Borg in *Star Trek* blend machine and human parts.

Geek Facts:

- Darth Vader is a cyborg, while Data from *Star Trek* is called an android. Johnny 5 from *Short Circuit* is a robot.

- The 1927 *Metropolis* features the first android in film.

- In 1999 a strike by robots shut down a Toyota manufacturing plant for two weeks.

- Brent Spiner, who played Data on *Star Trek: The Next Generation,* said that people would often come up to him and demand to look at his mechanical brain.

- Regis Philbin recently spent some time off, and was replaced by a cyborg on *Live with Regis and Kelly.*

- The Robot Defamation League requested that break-dancers rename "the robot" dance move to something else, because it was offensive to robots.

Movie Robot or Programming Language?

Can you tell which is a movie robot and which is a programming language?

1.	Gort	Robot	Language
2.	Robby	Robot	Language
3.	AMOS	Robot	Language
4.	NEXUS-6	Robot	Language
5.	Cecil	Robot	Language
6.	Guile	Robot	Language
7.	Proteus	Robot	Language
8.	Prolog	Robot	Language
9.	CHOMPS	Robot	Language
10.	M-MUMPS	Robot	Language
11.	Johnny 5	Robot	Language
12.	DARYL	Robot	Language
13.	Occam	Robot	Language
14.	Rexx	Robot	Language
15.	Cilk	Robot	Language

Swiss Army Knife

Geek Cred: The Swiss Army Knife, the tool of choice among geeks like MacGyver, is a pocketknife with many different attachments from a leather punch to a wine opener. Current models include USB drives and laser pointers. The original Swiss Army Knife was created in 1897 by Karl Elsener, the founder of the Victorinox company.

Geek Facts:

- The Swiss Army Knife is standard equipment on the space shuttle flights.

- In 2005 Victorinox acquired Wenger, once again reducing the number of manufacturers to one. However, both brands are active.

- The Eiffel Tower was built using only The Parisian model of Swiss Army Knife.

- In the never-aired *MacGyver* episode "Mac Goes Bananas," MacGyver slays thirty-two sorority members with his Spartan.

- A study showed that men with bigger Swiss Army Knives had bigger pockets in which to carry it around.

- The Russian space agency spent three million dollars building a multitool for their cosmonauts, while NASA spent $5 on a Swiss Army Knife. This is totally not an urban legend.

Top 11 Swiss Army Tools That Every Geek Needs

11. The Security Shield: Shields the knife from airport security so it can be taken on flights.

10. The Wi-Fi Seeker: Vibrates when a wireless Internet signal is available.

9. The Shrinker: Shrinks the knife with a few too many tools into a size that can comfortably fit in a pocket.

8. The Pwner: For use at LAN parties. Distracts other players with its shiny colors, allowing the user to pwn others.

7. The Time Reverser: For those times when you want to take back the three-minute rant you just went on about how George Lucas sucks while you're trying to pick up women.

6. The Enlarger: Makes a man's package look bigger than it really is.

5. The Battery Backup: Converts kinetic energy into electric energy to recharge all your gizmos.

4. The "That's a Knife" Blade: Blade that doubles in size when compared to any other Swiss Army Knife, for those times when you need a Crocodile Dundee reference.

3. The Laser Cauterizer: When you cut your fingers with the other tools on the knife.

2. The Mouse: Wireless mouse blade.

1. The Drainer: For siphoning excess caffeine from the blood, when one too many Red Bulls have been consumed.

Commodore 64

Geek Cred: The best-selling model of personal computer ever with over seventeen million units sold. The Commodore 64 (C64) was a great gaming machine for its time. At $595 it was a much better value for the power than other computers like the Apple II or the IBM PC.

Geek Facts:

- The peripheral market for the C64 was large and included products like a 10 MB hard drive and mouse. Some companies are still making devices for the C64.

- The C64 did not have a reset button installed, but users achieved resets by using a "reset cartridge" or by shorting out two pins on the system.

- If you typed POKE786, 13: SYS31337 into the C64, it would double the speed of the processor and allow you to connect to the Internet.

- The sleek design of the C64 case has been copied in such diverse areas as bludgeoning weapons and Tupperware containers.

- Fearing their system was being labeled as a "kid's game machine" Commodore released the adult-oriented Rear Admiral 69 computer system.

- Until smugglers obtained an Atari 520ST in 2004, the Commodore 64 was the most powerful computer available in Tajikistan.

Top 11 Signs You Have an Old Computer

11. It has blinking lights on it (that's actual lights, not LEDs).

10. The default spell-check dictionary is Olde English.

9. The noise insulation is made from asbestos.

8. It's too slow for the latest version of Nethack.

7. The memory is hand soldered onto the motherboard.

6. Eighty-column lines of text wrap to three lines.

5. Not even your parents want it.

4. The Smithsonian keeps calling to see if you'll donate it.

3. Green and amber are your only choices in monitors.

2. The CPU speed is measured in fractions of MHz.

1. It's made by Commodore Business Machines.

IBM

Geek Cred: IBM holds more patents than any other US technology company. The company designed the Deep Blue chess-playing computer that defeated chess champion Garry Kasparov in 1997, though Kasparov accused it of cheating.

Geek Facts:

- The IBM PC, which set the standard for years to come, debuted in 1981.

- The company changed its name to International Business Machines Corporation from the Computing-Tabulating-Recording Company in 1924.

- "You can't get fired for buying IBM," proved false for Henry Jacobs. As purchasing manager at Apple Computer, he replaced the company's Macs with IBM PCs to save money, and was promptly fired.

- IBM continues to refuse to license their patents on time travel, preventing production of commercial time machines.

- The nickname "Big Blue" comes from the fact that up until 1963, the company required members of its sales force to have "Big Blue" eyes and blond hair.

- New management has loosened the company's uptight business culture in recent years. For example, IBM now has "Orgy Fridays" twice a month.

IBM to Enter Business Gaming Console Market with System BF

ARMONK, NY — With experience from manufacturing chips for all current generation gaming consoles, IBM has decided to enter the relatively untapped business gaming console market with a console called "System BF."

"The BF stands for Business Fun," said head of IBM's newly created gaming division, Elijah Smalls. "All the current companies are focused on the home market, leaving the business market wide open. Businesspeople like to have fun too!"

The system, based on an updated version of the Xbox 360 chip, will come with the IBMote game controller. "This generation of gamers probably hasn't experienced what chiclet-style keys can do. We had plenty left over from our PC Jr. days, so we figured we'd use them up on the controllers," said Smalls.

Many wonder what companies will be buying a console gaming system for their employees, but Smalls isn't worried. Smalls pointed to a study that showed that workers were 45 percent more productive when allowed to game at work. "As far as competing with the Wii or Xbox in the business gaming market, I don't think any serious business would go there, I mean when we have games like Mavis Beacon Teaches Typing 84, then it's hard to compete with us."

Smalls said IBM's extensive array of launch games will include titles like Accounting Hero, Consultant's Creed, Sonic the Hedge Fund, and God of Mergers.

"And we don't have to worry about alienating our current customers. Microsoft said they would cooperate fully with us in this endeavor and I know we can trust them."

IBM stock was down on the news.

Charles Babbage

Geek Cred: Programming geeks have Babbage to thank. He developed the idea for the programmable computer. Not only that, but he invented the cowcatcher for trains, so cow-tipping geeks can thank him also. If that weren't enough, a video game store chose to name itself after him, which completes the geek trifecta.

Geek Facts:

- Like Hawking and Newton, he was the Lucasian Professor of Mathematics at Cambridge.

- A difference engine was built from his original plans and functioned properly.

- Babbage is also credited with creating the first "nerdcore rap" album, entitled *Straight Outta Oxford* with his group, Thug Differential.

- Babbage cemented his reputation as an eccentric by performing his "Symphony for the Flute and Flatulence" at a gala for the Queen.

- His chief rival in mathematics was the noted German mathematician Wolfgang Bettuce. Both had great heads for math.

- Babbage hated street musicians so much that he built a catapult to fling them across the Thames. He and his "boys" used it regularly.

Apple to Release "Portable" iDifference Engine

SAN FRANCISCO, CA – Steve Jobs at the latest MacWorld Conference announced that Apple is going retro with their latest gadget: the iDifference Engine.

Based on Charles Babbage's original plans, the iDifference Engine will easily fit into any living room or computer parlor. The concept may be retro, but the design is anything but. Babbage's original design has been tweaked to feature iPod's patented click-wheel and brushed metallic finish.

"At Apple we like to think different," said Jobs. "What's more different than the iDifference Engine? We're filling a need for our customers who like their polynomial functions calculated to an accuracy of thirty-one places. With the integrated click-wheel, customers won't tire cranking a massive handle that's common on other difference engines."

Critics argue that the functions of the iDifference Engine can be handled by a number of devices already on the market that weigh less than three thousand pounds.

"Apple customers have been willing to pay a premium for limited functionality as long as it's pretty," said Jobs. "We think they'll stick with us on the iDifference Engine."

Many Apple fans were excited by the announcement. "I don't know who Charles Babbage was, or what the hell a difference engine does, but I'm getting one," said Grant Markley of San Jose, California.

Jobs also previewed the next in line for retro-computing, the one-beaded iBacus, to the "oohs and ahs" of the crowd.

iPod

Geek Cred: Apple's iPod is the most widely used digital media player. The first iPods went on sale in 2001; now over 100 million have been sold. The gadget has transformed the digital entertainment market and made Apple a dominant player in the media industry.

Geek Facts:

- The first generation of iPods was available with 5 or 10 GB hard drives, which are tiny compared to current models.

- Apple has teamed with automobile manufacturers so that most new models of cars are "iPod compatible."

- Apple makes a bulletproof, Kevlar-coated iPod for soldiers in the U.S. Army. These special iPods still scratch easily.

- Rumors that pink iPod Nanos are coated with a chemical that can make you gay are completely true.

- Steve Jobs prefers Microsoft's Zune to his iPod.

- Fifth-generation iPods contain an Easter Egg which, when activated, unlocks the entire catalog of The Beatles on the iPod. To access these hidden songs, press "Menu-Menu-Play-Back-Forward-Back-Forward."

Apple Store to Begin Charging Entrance Fee

CUPERTINO, CA — If you want to see the iPhone at an Apple store, be sure to bring some cash. Large crowds flocking to see the next-generation iPhone and the MacBook Air have forced Apple to begin charging a $5 entrance fee for Apple stores. Many analysts anticipated the move, and expect a positive response from customers.

"Part of the move was to limit crowds to keep the stores safe, but also we wanted to keep the right kind of people in the stores," said vice president of retail outlets, Vince Sciopiano. "By 'right kind of people' I mean true Apple customers with money, willing to pay just to look at our newest wares."

While Apple Geniuses patrol inside the store, Apple "Muscleheads" will guard the window displays and entrances. For the $5 fee, customers will get an Apple button that will allow them entrance into the store and which is used to track the customer's movements. Sciopiano noted that the $5 fee could be applied to purchases on that visit.

Customer reaction at a pilot project at the Apple Store in Canoga Park, California was positive. Alexander Hu, an avid Mac user, said, "I don't mind paying to get into the store if it keeps out the iPhone gawkers and Windows lusers who want to drool over the new Macs."

Not everyone was pleased, though. Kyle Martin said, "Five dollars to just walk into the store? It's like they want to be elite snobs or something."

When told of the criticism, Sciopiano said, "That's exactly the case."

Transistor

Geek Cred: The invention of the transistor brought forth the modern electronic era. The reliability and miniaturization allowed by transistors made possible the computers and gadgets that geeks love.

Geek Facts:

- Many consider the transistor to be the greatest invention of the twentieth century.

- Shockley, Bardeen, and Brattain received the Nobel Prize in Physics for their discovery of the transistor.

- Several names were considered for the device including Shockley's Shocker, the Crusher of Souls, and Mini Voltamatic Switcher, before "transistor" was chosen.

- The engineers at Bell Labs were actually trying to develop a chewing gum that wouldn't lose its flavor when they stumbled upon the transistor.

- Most computer science majors don't know how a transistor works and consider it to be "magic."

- Some types of transistors include the MOSFET, FinFET, and BOBAFETT.

Amish Engineer Develops Quad-Core Vacuum Tube Processor

LANCASTER, PA — Ishmael Gruntl, an Amish engineer working at Intel, has used advances in vacuum tube technology to develop a quad-core processor.

Gruntl, part of the New New Order of Amish, which allows some technology, but not the latest, like transistors, was employed by Intel as part of their outreach program to try to create better computers using older technology. Before the transistor, most computers relied on the unreliable vacuum tube, but the technology has faded except in some niche areas.

Gruntl was excited by his advance. "Now with punch cards and some blinking lights we can calculate the yields of our crops much more accurately than we could before."

Gruntl's Amish order allows technology as long as it's at least a generation behind the current one. Gruntl's advances have decreased the power requirements for vacuum tubes, allowing lower heat dissipation and more tubes to be packed on a board. His quad-core processor works at .015 MHz.

"It would be great if we could use some sort of display," said Gruntl, "but the Grand Council hasn't approved that technology yet."

Intel reps said they expect to sell three to four of the processors to Amish farmers and furniture manufacturers. "We'll load these systems with a punch card version of Quickbooks so they can track their income and expenses better."

Dremel Rotary Tool

Geek Cred: The tool of choice for hardware geeks. Nothing is more fun than modifying your toys, and to do this you need a versatile tool. Cutting a hole in the side of your computer case? Modifying your Tickle Me Elmo? The high-speed rotary tool has lots of attachments for various jobs, from drilling and cutting to sanding and routing.

Geek Facts:

- The Dremel Company was founded in 1932 in Racine, Wisconsin, by Albert J. Dremel.

- Over 17 million rotary tools are in use today with over 150 bits to use.

- The least successful Dremel bit was the razor sharp nose hair trimmer that removed 2,500 noses before it was discontinued.

- The Dremel Cult of Toronto, Ontario, believes that a giant Dremel tool at the North Pole is responsible for the rotation of the Earth.

- During World War II in France, one soldier held off a troop of German soldiers from his underground position using only duct tape and a Dremel tool, allowing the rest of his troop to escape.

- The most popular attachment among women is the Dremel Power Pleaser.

Geek Parents Using Cooling Technology Instead of Medicine to Lower Fevers

ANN ARBOR, MI – Geeks familiar with using technology to solve their problems have turned to advanced cooling solutions instead of pharmaceuticals to lower fevers in their children.

"My daughter came down with a 103-degree fever," said Fernando Ferringer of coolingyourkids.com. "I knew we didn't have any Tylenol, and that's when I had a 'Eureka' moment."

Ferringer connected a water-cooling system and a couple of heat sinks to his daughter to reduce her fever. "I figured the system cools down my CPU, which runs hotter than my daughter. Why couldn't it cool her down? She did scream a bit when her hair got tangled in the fan, but we took care of that."

Ferringer set up his Web site to share his knowledge with others. "I'm always hoping my kids will get sick, so I can try out something new," he said.

Young parents familiar with the Internet and computers have flocked to the site. "Lots of bad things can happen when you give your kids medicine, like barfing up grape-flavored Motrin. I feel much better smearing thermal paste on their forehead and strapping on a Zalman," said Kurt Ullery of Indianapolis.

Ferringer does not recommend taking a Dremel to your kids and putting Lexan panels or neon lights in them. "Those are just for show and really aren't necessary for cooling or performance," he said.

Rube Goldberg Machine

Final step: Getting the writer to write

Geek Cred: A Rube Goldberg machine is an overly complicated device that performs a simple task. Usually the machine will proceed in steps to make progress towards the goal. Goldberg got a degree in engineering from UC Berkeley, and his cartoons of comical machines have inspired generations of geeks to replicate them in real life.

Geek Facts:

- Other countries have different names for the Rube Goldberg machine, such as in the U.K. where it is known as a Heath Robinson machine after a British cartoonist.

- Goldberg earned a Pulitzer Prize for his political cartooning.

- The most complex Rube Goldberg machine to date is the engine of the Toyota Prius.

- According to historians, a shot from a Rube Goldberg machine killed Archduke Ferdinand and precipitated World War I.

- The first mention of a Rube Goldberg–type machine occurs in the Bible. God swings a golf club and after a series of events a mule kicks over a bucket of water, causing it to rain for forty days and forty nights.

- In Japan a Rube Goldberg machine is known as an Urkel.

Wacky CIA Operative Developed Rube Goldberg Torture Devices

GUANTANAMO BAY, CUBA – New pictures from the detention facilities at Guantanamo Bay reveal that intricate machines are being used to interrogate suspected terrorists.

Abel Consforth, a CIA operative, has come forward to take credit for the machines. "I'm really proud of the devices I've made," said Consforth. "I love the waterboarding one. The bowling ball knocks over the fishing rod, which makes the hamster run, which rolls up the string that tips over the bucket that pours water over the suspect's face. Just awesome."

Consforth said his superiors didn't authorize the devices, but it was his own American ingenuity and initiative that made it possible. "Interrogations were getting boring, so I came up with ways to make them more exciting. The anticipation of the prisoner as the machine progresses is so much better this way."

Consforth also demonstrated his device for shocking prisoners with a cattle prod. "My favorite part of that one is when the marble knocks over the dominoes, which let loose the mouse for the cat to chase. Then the umbrella falls on the cat, making him squeal, which frightens the parakeet, which lets loose the cattle prod."

Videos of the devices have been circulating on YouTube for several weeks now. Consforth has been placed on administrative leave while the incidents are investigated.

"I don't see what the big deal is," said Consforth. "There's nothing in the Geneva Conventions banning Rube Goldberg machines."

A representative from Amnesty International chuckled while watching the videos. "You have to commend the ingeniousness of the devices, but we still contend this is torture."

Intel

Geek Cred: Founded in 1968 by Gordon Moore (of Moore's Law fame) and Bob Noyce (coinventor of the integrated circuit), Intel is the world's largest semiconductor company. It created the x86 series of microprocessors that power a majority of personal computers.

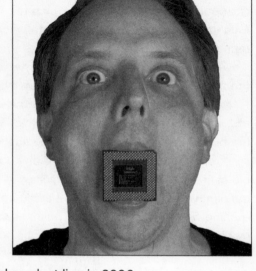

Geek Facts:

- Apple finally converted to an all-Intel product line in 2006.

- Intel's fourth employee was Andy Grove, who was the company's CEO during the high-growth period from 1987 to 1998.

- Intel's corporate culture is much less relaxed than other Silicon Valley companies, and actually forbids employees to smile except on "Smile Wednesdays."

- The "86" in the "x86" processor comes from the number of times the inventor of the chip saw the movie *Star Wars*.

- Contrary to popular opinion, Intel never considered calling the successor to the Pentium the Sextium. However, Schlongium did make the final cut.

- There have only been two confirmed cases of Intel chips becoming so hot they've melted through to the core of the Earth. Reports of six other such events were uncovered as fakes.

Microsoft and Intel Outline Future of Computing: Can't Do Shit

REDMOND, WA – At a technology conference for developers, representatives from Microsoft and Intel outlined the Can't Do Shit (CDS) Road Map for future cooperative products between the two companies. They predict that in six years it will be impossible to violate a copyright with a computer, or to do anything at all for that matter.

"We're very confident that with the release of our Windows 7 platform and Intel's Octocore processors none of consumers' previous digital media will work. No MP3s, no movie files, nothing," said Josiah Witman of Microsoft. "The following year we plan to release a new version of Office that will be unable to function with any files created by previous versions, thus furthering the CDS initiative greatly."

Intel foresees a similar path. "Our Octocore processor will make sure that any digital media is completely inaccessible without paying a fee. The next generation of processors will perform at double the speed, but will be incapable of outputting any video signals. If consumers can bypass Microsoft's content-protection system, we have to make sure they can't utilize it in any way," said Harold Gresler of Intel.

Developers agreed that the future of computing is not being able to do shit. "I can't wait to start developing for the CDS platform. You give the customer control of the computer and they just screw things up," said Tom Robbins of Plusex Designs. "It's better to make sure they can't do shit. Then you've got stability."

Many consumers agreed, "I think Microsoft and Intel are moving very quickly with this new plan, because I'm already at the point where I can't do shit with their products."

AMD

Geek Cred: AMD brought competition to the dominant Intel in the CPU market. AMD gained most of its credibility by creating 64-bit processors that outperformed Intel's offerings. AMD has appealed to enthusiasts because of their embracing of over-clocking.

Geek Facts:

- AMD beat Intel to 1 GHz by releasing the 1 GHz Athlon a couple of days before Intel released the 1 GHz Pentium III.

- AMD's first microprocessor was a reverse-engineered 8080A standard processor.

- Following the naming conventions of their previous Athlon and Duron processors, AMD released the Moron processor in 2000.

- In 2001, AMD started rating chips in the proprietary "GiggaHertz" unit to give the appearance of higher clock speed. One GiggaHertz was equal to 500 MHz.

- The flamboyant Jerry Sanders kept AMD afloat during tough times with money he earned as a Kenny Rogers impersonator in Las Vegas.

- In 2003 AMD ended support for their Socket 666 processors, after intense lobbying by Christian groups.

AMD, ATI Merge to Form DAAMIT

SUNNYVALE, CA – AMD CEO Hector Ruiz said that with the merger of AMD and ATI the new company would be called DAAMIT.

"We wanted to keep the letters from each company, but didn't like the looks of AMDATI. It lacks imagination. Our marketing team found that 'DAAMIT' appealed most to our focus groups," said Ruiz.

Ruiz noted that DAAMIT is an ancient Incan word meaning "fleet of foot, speedy" and that's the "kind of company that we want to be."

Customers were pleased by the move. "That's what I usually say when I load new drivers on my system, so it seems appropriate," said Kyle Westfall of Wausau, Wisconsin.

When asked if the company would continue its focus on the gaming market Ruiz said, "Yes, if people think of gaming, we want them to think DAAMIT!"

Rumors that DAAMIT will make fully integrated computers not compatible with third-party hardware brought threats of litigation from Apple for patent infringement.

DAAMIT's stock was down on the news.

Steve Wozniak

Geek Cred: Woz is the hardware genius who developed the first Apple computer and was one of the company's cofounders, along with Steve Jobs. Woz, a typical computer geek, is annoyed by his level of celebrity. He ran a Dial-a-Joke line out of his house.

Geek Facts:

- In 2000 he was inducted into the National Inventors Hall of Fame.

- Wozniak crashed his plane and as a result suffered from amnesia and did not remember the crash or his following hospital stay.

- Wozniak eats his weight in Polish sausage every day to keep his athletic physique.

- If you press open-Apple J-O-B on an Apple IIe, the computer will beep the "Imperial March" from *Star Wars*.

- In 1981 Wozniak made a primitive iPod using only parts from a Fry Daddy and a transistor radio.

- Always a fan of pulling pranks, Wozniak once sent Bill Gates the severed head of a horse.

How Does Steve Wozniak Spend His Day?

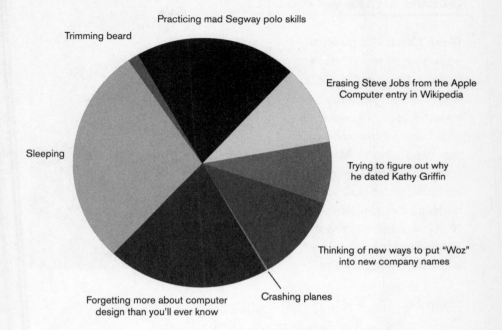

Steve Jobs

Geek Cred: The question wasn't whether to include Steve Jobs or not, it was where to put him. Jobs could've easily fit under the software or the movies pillars, too. In addition to Apple, Jobs started NeXT Computer and developed hardware and software including the NeXTstep operating system. Advanced for its time, but sales never materialized.

Geek Facts:

- Jobs bought Pixar from Lucasfilm in 1986.

- Jobs once worked as a technician at Atari.

- Jobs is not a vegan, but he only eats human meat from employees who miss deadlines.

- Apple fans may think Jobs can walk on water; he can't. He can levitate over solid ground, though.

- Always a fan of Eastern culture and thought, Steve Jobs bought the country of Sri Lanka with the proceeds of his sale of Apple stock.

- Jobs feels most comfortable in a black turtleneck, because he paid his way through college working as a mime.

Apple Faithful Ready "Oohs," "Aahs"
for Jobs Keynote

SAN FRANCISCO, CA – Hundreds of Apple enthusiasts gathered in a warehouse outside of San Francisco practicing their "Oohs" and "Aahs" for the upcoming keynote address by Apple CEO Steve Jobs.

"I really want to get in this year," said Kevin Starnick who was denied access last year because his "Aahs" didn't pass muster with Apple security and marketing.

Soaring expectations fueled by the Apple marketing machine have prompted fierce competition among emoters. No one wants to be left behind and miss what almost 5 percent of the computing population will be talking about tomorrow.

Gregory Simons, head of the local Ooh-Aah Squad, uses tapes of previous keynote speeches to hone his team's skills. "This year Jobs is gonna be blown away by our awe," said Simons. "Disappointment will not prevent us from performing our duty. No matter what's unveiled, we're still going to make sure He knows we're impressed."

There was a palpable excitement in the warehouse just one day away from the keynote, but not everyone was as sanguine as the head Ooh-Aaher.

"I know this might cost me my spot in the audience, but I'm just not feeling it this year," said Charles Duprey. "Before past conventions I couldn't sleep for days. Now I'm getting a good eight hours. I think my hype quota has been exhausted."

Overall, however, the feelings were positive and were best summed up by a very enthusiastic member. "I really hope it's that One-Button Keyboard that we've been hearing rumors about, then I won't have to fake it!"

The Ooh-Aah Squad denied any connection to Apple's Royal Order of the Noses of Brown organization.

Moore's Law

Geek Cred: Moore's Law states that the number of transistors on an integrated circuit doubles every two years. It was an observation made by Intel founder Gordon Moore in 1965 that concerns the number of transistors on a chip. It has been modified slightly since the original observation.

Geek Facts:

■ Moore has since noted that the law cannot continue indefinitely; eventually the law of exponentials will make it impossible.

■ Moore's Law corresponds to a 1 percent improvement per week.

■ Moore's Law is not related to Gordon (Freemans)'s Law which states that the number of headcrabs that appear will outnumber your ammo by one.

■ Employees at Intel found breaking Moore's Law must use a computer with a 486SX CPU for a week.

■ In 1993 Intel was accused of putting in extra transistors that didn't do anything, just to keep up with the law.

■ The lounge for Intel hardware engineers, who are forced to comply with Moore's Law, contains a dartboard with Gordon Moore's face on it.

Top 11 Other Moore's Laws

11. Moore's Law for Internet Morons—The number of morons on the Internet doubles every eighteen months.

10. Moore's Law for the RIAA—The stupidity of the RIAA's lawsuits double every eighteen months.

9. Moore's Law for Days in a Month—The number of days in a month stays at approximately thirty every eighteen months.

8. Moore's Law of World of Warcraft—The number of nubs and gold farmers on a server doubles every eighteen months.

7. Moore's Law for Internet Memes—Every Internet meme will be double posted every eighteen months.

6. Moore's Law for Moore's Law—the number of Moore's Laws for things will double every eighteen months.

5. Roger Moore's Law—Bond will Double-0 7 every eighteen months.

4. Moore's Law for Blog Hype—Blog hype for the "next big thing" will double every eighteen months.

3. Moore's LOL of LOLcats—I can haz doubling?

2. S'mores Law—Your weight will double in eighteen months if all you eat is s'mores.

1. Moore's Law of Spare Computer Parts—Space needed to store old computer parts will need to double every eighteen months.

Overclocking

Geek Cred: When you spend as much on technology as geeks do, you want to get the most out of your money. Overclocking is the practice of running a computer component at faster than its labeled speed. Overclocking a computer can lead to instability or destruction of the computer component because of overheating.

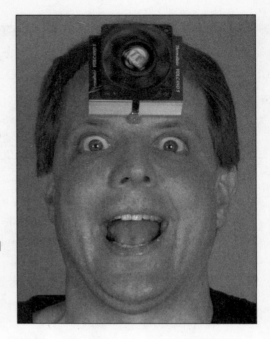

Geek Facts:

- While overclocking generally applies to a CPU and video chips, other components can be overclocked as well.

- Many AMD CPUs can be unlocked by drawing a trace between pins using conductive paint or a pencil lead.

- The time it takes for all the cards to bounce away after a Solitaire victory is often used as a benchmark during overclocking experiments.

- AMD lowered the labeled speed on their Extreme OC line of processors so they could claim better overclocking results.

- Mayonnaise mixed with Grey Poupon mustard makes an excellent thermal paste as well as a tasty sandwich spread.

- "Overclocking—the Cologne" was released in 2003, but the scent of smoke and burning plastic proved to be unpopular.

Overclocked Jesus Performs Miracles Faster

CHICAGO, IL – Chicago students Goran Radovich and Trey Gafney over-clocked Jesus, so that he now performs miracles nearly twice as fast as before.

"We had a spare Jesus sitting around, so we got out the Jesus and cranked up the clock," said Gafney. "He started sweating pretty profusely at about 2.5 GHz, so we went out and got the hose to spray him down."

"When we got him up to about 3.75 GHz, we started having some problems like that hole in Tommy's abdomen and the sudden change of seasons," said Radovich. "After that, we clocked him down and he was stable most of the time at 3.69 GHz.

"We had all the bread and fish and wine that we ever needed," continued Radovich, "and we both had straight A's, so we took him down to the hospital to do some more miracles there. We turned him on and his arms were flying around and deaf people could hear, the crippled could walk. Of course, a couple of times he got going too fast and a blind guy got an extra eye."

The young men explained that they expect to get Jesus saving people even faster when they figure out how to safely immerse him in liquid nitrogen.

INTERNET

ARPANET

Geek Cred: ARPANET was the network that eventually became the Internet. It was developed by DARPA of the U.S. Department of Defense. The idea of the project was to connect the large computers in the country so that researchers in remote locations could use the computers.

Geek Facts:

- ARPANET was not designed with the intent of withstanding a nuclear attack. It just needed to be a reliable network in case some machines went down.

- The first ARPANET connection was made in January of 1969.

- The first message sent across the network was "FIRST POST!!!!" by BBN engineer Thomas Trolle.

- Being 1969, most of the computer problems had to do with the computers smoking pot.

- J. C. R. Licklider, who developed many of the ideas which led to ARPANET, said, "Someday technology historians will look back at my accomplishments and laugh at my name."

- Within thirty-six hours of creation of the ARPANET, the first ASCII porn image was transmitted, foreshadowing the main purpose of the Internet.

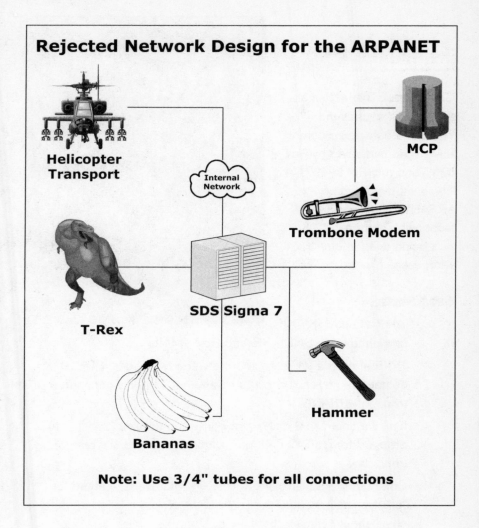

Rejected Network Design for the ARPANET

Helicopter Transport

Internal Network

MCP

Trombone Modem

T-Rex

SDS Sigma 7

Hammer

Bananas

Note: Use 3/4" tubes for all connections

Email

Geek Cred: The first email system that could send messages between different hosts was developed by Ray Tomlinson of BBN in 1971. It was implemented on the ARPANET. Tomlinson was responsible for the "@" sign being used in email addresses.

Geek Facts:

- The first email programs were SNDMSG and READMAIL.

- The first messages were sent between two Digital PDP10 computers physically next to each other, but only connected through ARPANET.

- If all the spam sent daily were converted to razor blades and dropped from a 747 on top of all the spammers, it would be a great day.

- Contrary to popular belief, the "e" in email doesn't stand for "electronic," it stands for "English," which is the language all email should officially be sent in.

- Originally, Tomlinson wanted to use the smiley:-) instead of the "@" symbol to separate the user from the domain, but he thought it was too cutesy.

- It's not known exactly what was in the first email, but the last email sent will be "So long and thanks for all the fish."

Top 11 Reasons You Shouldn't Forward Me That Email

11. I eat puppies, kittens, and other cute animals, and sending me pictures of them only makes me hungry for more.

10. I've been on the Internet forever and have already seen/heard/smelled whatever you're sending.

9. You'd like me to remain your friend.

8. I don't care if the kid dies from cancer.

7. I have a sense of humor and that joke isn't remotely funny.

6. If you forward that message to ten of your friends, then a unicorn dies.

5. You'll prove once and for all that I'm smarter than you.

4. I am actually hoping to get robbed/mugged/carjacked.

3. If I wanted to see pictures of babies, I'd buy an Anne Geddes book.

2. If it doesn't have to do with making my penis bigger, then I don't want it in my Inbox.

1. Bill Gates already sent me my free Xbox 360, $1,000, and tickets to Disneyland. I don't want to be greedy.

Bulletin Board Systems

Geek Cred: During the 1980s and early 1990s, before the dawn of the World Wide Web, geeks would dial into local Bulletin Board Systems (BBS) to interact online. A BBS is a computer with a modem running one of the myriad BBS programs. Operated by a Systems Operator (SysOp) BBSes were places to post messages, play games, chat, and upload and download files.

Geek Facts:

- One of the most notable BBSes is The WELL, which has been one of the few to transform itself into a Web presence.

- The first BBS software was CBBS, created by Ward Christensen in 1978.

- AOL still uses the XMODEM protocol for some of their dial-up services.

- Phone phreak Captain Crunch could log on to his favorite BBS by whistling into the phone.

- The collapse of BBSes after the emergence of the WWW also meant the demise of ASCII porn companies such as ASCII Angels and Playdot.

- BBS systems are still very popular in North Korea, but most are used to trade grains of rice.

Old Guy on Message Board Won't Shut Up About Ancient Technology

Message posters on the techgeeknow.com message board can't get a user named "SomeOldGuy" to shut up about the old days of technology, increasingly causing tension among the users.

Blake Forwich, who posts under the name CapnApollo, said, "I made a post complaining about my DSL service, and SomeOldGuy starts talking about how he had a 300 baud acoustic coupler modem. I didn't even know what the hell that is. I had to look it up on Wikipedia."

Other contributors to the board had similar complaints. Lyle Gorzinski, who posts under the name Lylezilla, said, "He's always talking about how it was back in the BBS days, and how only one person was on the board at a time. How he'd have to dial for hours just to get through. I mean, who cares? It's the twenty-first century now."

SomeOldGuy is George Coltz, a fifty-four-year-old technical documentation writer from Peoria, Illinois. He thinks kids these days don't appreciate where all this technology came from. "Keyboards? Monitors? My first computer used punch cards and blinking lights. I take some time to educate these kids about the past and all they do is get me banned from the board."

Frank Borden, who runs the board, said, "I banned him once, but he begged me to let him back on. He said he'd only talk about current technology. I felt sorry for him and let him back on. Next thing I know he's talking about Gopher and XMODEM. Can't teach an old dog, I guess."

SETI@Home

Geek Cred: SETI@Home uses Internet-connected computers to Search for Extraterrestrial Intelligence (SETI). Geeks download a free program that analyzes radio telescope data to search for signs of aliens.

Geek Facts:

- A worker in Ohio was fired in 2004 for loading the SETI program on state computers to try to get more work units completed.

- The first modern SETI project occurred in 1960 at Cornell University using a twenty-five-meter radio telescope.

- One inventive student at Carnegie Mellon University created a way to analyze SETI data using only duct tape and an eight-sided die.

- No intelligent signals have been found, but several lost episodes of *The Jeff Foxworthy Show* were discovered.

- The least successful distributed computing project was the "Search for the Phone Number of that Girl that Kinda Liked Me" started by an engineering student at the University of Texas in 2002.

- Scientists thought they had found an alien signal in 2003, but, according to the Air Force, it was just a weather balloon.

RIAA Donates to SETI; Hopes to Sue Aliens

LOS ANGELES, CA – The SETI@Home project, which uses unused processing power from home computers to analyze radio telescope data to search for alien intelligence, has received a large donation from an unlikely source—the RIAA.

According to RIAA representative Larry Grant, the move is part public relations and part research and development. "We hope to improve our image with many Internet users by funding such a popular project," said Grant, "but also we hope to find another source of income."

Grant explained that broadcast signals travel forever, so it is likely that an alien civilization is picking up broadcasts of RIAA artists. "If they're picking up a broadcast, then they are probably recording the songs and sharing them illegally."

Currently, U.S. copyright laws don't extend into space, but Congress is moving to extend them into the known universe.

"We're not interfering with the project in any way. We just want first crack at suing the aliens when they are found," said Grant. "Just think of it. When the aliens finally figure out what they are doing is illegal, it will be thousands of years later. A thousand years' worth of copyright violations? Those judgments will be astronomical!"

Many scientists on the project think that suing an alien culture might not be the best strategy for "first contact." However, they feel it's better than the government's plan of bombing the aliens, so they've accepted the RIAA's offer.

Tim Berners-Lee

Geek Cred: Geeks know there's a difference between the Internet and the World Wide Web. If you need someone to explain it to you, then just ask Tim Berners-Lee, who invented the Web and created the first Web browser. He now heads the World Wide Web Consortium (W3C) which attempts to set standards for the Web.

Geek Facts:

- The first Web site was put online at CERN in August of 1991.
- Berners-Lee won the Millennium Technology Prize in 2004 for inventing the Web.
- Berners-Lee designed the Web in 1971 using sticks, string, clay, and some burlap sacks. It took twenty years before his vision was realized on computers.
- The first Web site created was a big, blinking "FREE KEVIN!"
- The early days of the Web were dangerous for designers. Until size limitations were implemented in 1993, sites that were too large would cause computers to explode.
- Berners-Lee doesn't make any money from his idea of the Web, choosing to make it freely available for anyone to use and so ensuring its spread. However, if you send this page to ten friends, Bill Gates will send you $5.

World Wide Web Consortium Announces
New Features for CSS3

After years of development, the World Wide Web Consortium (W3C) has announced some of the exciting new features in Cascading Style Sheets, CSS3.

"We've been focusing a lot on the accessibility of Style Sheets," Darren Stennet, chief developer at W3C, explained. "CSS has been around for many years and is supported by nearly every single browser. So why don't people use them? Judging from most pages out there, we figured that CSS has simply been too complicated for the average user."

To solve this, W3C introduced a new class: "Template." This class allows web designers to define the entire layout of their site, using only a single line of CSS.

"We expect templates to become a hit," Darren Stennet exclaimed. "With only a single line of code (such as "template {aol; nauseating}"), designers can make the same mind-numbingly ugly sites that used to take them hours to make. Heck, they'll probably get even uglier."

Stennet promised that the dreaded Internet Explorer padding bug has been addressed. "Some of us suggested that we should let Microsoft have their way, but our solution will make everyone happy: CSS will support a new type of padding: padding_outside_of_the_friggin_element. Let's see them mess that one up."

Browser developers welcomed the new features. Mozilla developers announced, "It's already implemented in the latest Beta—we'll have it out by next week. IE sucks."

The word from Opera is, "Bertil is milking the goats right now. When he is done, he will do the code. Then we will have some nice goat cheese. Mmmmmmm."

Microsoft expects to have it ready "somewhere around IE8."

Nigerian Spam

Geek Cred: If you have an email address that's been active for more than ten minutes, you're likely to have seen scam letters from people claiming to be rich and in desperate circumstances. Many geeks enjoy turning the tables on the scammers, making them take pictures of themselves in compromising situations.

Geek Facts:

- Though no geek would fall for the scam, many people still lose millions of dollars every year to the scammers.

- If you've fallen for the scam, you're a "mugu," which is why the scam is sometimes referred to as "mugu mail."

- In 1775 Benjamin Franklin received a letter from what appeared to be a Nigerian king that wanted Franklin to hold his fortune of $1,000. Franklin was not duped, and wrote about it in his autobiography.

- The Congressional Budget Office estimates that 2 percent of the national debt can be attributed to various U.S. presidents falling for the Nigerian scams.

- The U.S. Secret Service, who prosecutes the crimes, suggests that recipients of the scam emails print out the message and burn them. That way scammers cannot get your email address.

- A 1998 law requiring all scammers to send their messages using an @scam.com email address for easy filtering never caught on with the scammers.

Nigerian Billionaire Can't Give Away Money

LAGOS, NIGERIA — Nigerian oil billionaire Esenam Ayele wants to share his millions with the rest of the world, but he's having trouble finding takers.

"Charities use too much of my donations in overhead, so I've been contacting people through email and asking if they want to share in my wealth. I thought it would be easy to give away millions and make it on the Top 100 Philanthropists list, but I have only had one taker so far," explained Ayele.

Thomas Hutton of St. Louis, Missouri, was the lucky recipient of $12 million from Ayele. "I was so excited when I received this email from Ayele. I mean, how many times do you get to help out a Nigerian billionaire? Since then I've gotten a lot more opportunities that I'm going to check out."

Ayele is furious at the countless Nigerian scammers who flood the Internet with messages hoping for an easy mark. "These people make my job more difficult. That is why I've started the Society of Charitable African Millionaires organization. This group of wealthy Africans finds ways to fight the spammers, so legitimate philanthropists can share their money with random people through the miracle of the Internet."

Ayele has encouraged SCAM members to proudly proclaim their SCAM membership in their emails, so the SCAM name can become a sign of trust. "I sign each email with 'Proud to be a SCAMmer,' but unfortunately my success rate has gone down since. What can I do?" wondered Ayele.

Kevin Mitnick

Geek Cred: Probably the most well-known criminal hacker, but not the most dangerous. There's no doubt that Mitnick did illegal things, but the extent of his exploits are a matter of debate. Mitnick was held in jail as a flight risk for four years without bail or charges brought against him, which spawned the "Free Kevin" movement.

Geek Facts:

- Mitnick was held in solitary confinement, because officials thought he was so dangerous he could hack into computers by whistling into a pay phone.
- Mitnick now runs a computer security firm.
- Mitnick could not hack into a computer by whistling into a pay phone, but he could hypnotize prison guards by playing his kazoo.
- Of all the identities Mitnick used, his favorite was "Dick Dongbanger of Rockhard, Arkansas."
- Mitnick was known as "The Condor," because he could fly and liked to eat dead animals he found on the road.
- Kevin Mitnick just stole your credit card number.

Virus Writer's Mom Makes Him Apologize
to Everyone

ANN ARBOR, MI — Justin Rayburn, the fifteen-year-old author of the Gold-bear email virus that clogged computer networks last week, was forced to apologize in writing to all his victims. Unfortunately, the apology sends itself to everyone in a victim's address book, and has now surpassed the original virus as the top threat on the Internet.

"This is the first time we've ever seen a virus writer attempt to atone for his transgressions, so we were caught completely unawares," admitted Symantec spokesman Allan Geddis.

In fact, Geddis said Symantec has sent out numerous advisories in the past twelve hours urging users not to accept the apology, which read:

Dear Outlook Express user,

I'm really sorry I screwed up your computer with my virus. My mom is making me do this, so you can trust me this time and click on the attachment. It will disinfect your computer, honest! It'll also patch your computer, so I can never do this again.

Maryanne Rayburn, Justin's mother, said she discovered only two days ago in IRC that her son was the author of Goldbear. "He was raised a good Catholic, so his first response was to cover it up, but I wouldn't allow it," said Rayburn. "I told Justin that I don't care if it is the cool thing to do, he can't go around bringing down the entire Internet just because all his friends are doing it. I mean really, if all his friends started using Outlook Express, would he do that, too?"

Slashdot

Geek Cred: While it's called "News for Nerds," the lines are so blurred these days that geeks visit it as well. It's a news discussion site that focuses on topics of interest to most geeks, though its scope has broadened in recent years. Rob Malda and Jeff Bates run it, but now it has a much larger staff and expanded sections.

Geek Facts:

- Slashdot was created in September 1997.

- The 10,000,000th user comment was posted in August of 2004.

- Originally, the domain name was going to be used as a slash fiction site about the relationships between punctuation marks.

- Bill Gates has listed Slashdot as one of his favorite sites. He posts often in comment threads defending Microsoft under the nickname The_Zombie_Gates.

- The Slashdot trolling culture is so evolved that the department of anthropology at the University of California, Berkeley, teaches a class about it.

- From 2001 to 2003 the CIA used front-page links on Slashdot to shut down many sites suspected of supporting terrorist organizations.

Linux Kernel Delayed by Microsoft's Army
of Evil Monkeys

AROUND THE WORLD – Linus Torvalds announced yesterday on the "News for Nerds" site Slashdot that the Linux Kernel 2.8 will be delayed. He blamed the delay on interference from Microsoft's Army of Evil Monkeys. The army has been disrupting the lives of key Linux programmers, and in some cases destroying portions of code. Torvalds himself has been a victim of several Evil Monkey attacks.

Steve Ballmer denied any involvement by Microsoft in the matter. "We did receive the Army of Evil Monkeys when we purchased evil from Satan, but those monkeys are only temporary employees and not actual employees of Microsoft. Whatever they do on their own time is their own business."

If the accusations are proven true, this could force the Justice Department to reopen its antitrust case against Microsoft. "This could be one more example of how Microsoft is using its monopoly power and control of an Evil Monkey army to stifle competition," said U.S. Attorney Chet Webster.

"It has been horrible," said Linux programmer Rob Timmons, "the evil monkeys were everywhere. Trashing my computer, [defecating] in my bed. I lost several days' worth of work."

Internal Microsoft emails obtained by reporters tell of a secret monkey training ground where monkeys learn to seek out and harass Linux programmers. The only comments from Bill Gates have been, "Fly my pretty, fly!"

Geek Speak

Geek Cred: If you're going to be a true geek on the Internet, you must understand many different languages. From leet speak to chat acronyms, you must know the slang and clichés that power the Web. From ROFLMAO to AYBABTU, if you can't speak the speak, then you can't geek the geek.

Geek Facts:

- Asian emoticons are created so the reader can see the smiley without turning their heads ^_^ compared to the western :-).

- The "All your base are belong to us" cliché comes from the Japanese video game *Zero Wing*.

- The FBI has employed several twelve-year-old cryptographers fluent in leet speak to track communications of domestic terror cells using the code.

- LOLcats can be traced back to ancient Egyptian drawings of cats with hieroglyphics that roughly translate to: "I can haz pyramidz?"

- Because of China's reverence for Chairman Mao, the use of ROFLMAO has been banned in China.

- Members of the U.S. Congress have begun invoking Godwin's Law and ending debate at the mention of Hitler or Nazis.

Hour Lost Explaining Computer Terms

AUSTIN, TX — Josh Granger lost an hour of his life yesterday as he tried to explain the difference between memory and hard drive space to his mother, Cynthia Granger. The discussion started when Cynthia asked, "Will I have enough memory if I install this family-tree-maker software?"

What follows is the beginning of that "Lost Hour," as it has become known to Josh.

"Mom, it's not memory on a hard drive, it's storage capacity, and loading a program on your hard drive doesn't have anything to do with your memory," said Josh.

"But I only have 64 Em-Bee of R-A-M," said Cynthia, "and this program says it requires 85 Em-Bee. It says it requires a modem, too. Do we have a modem?"

"Yes, we have a 56K modem. And no, 64 MB RAM and 85 MB space on your hard drive is different, Mom. Just because they both are measured in megabytes doesn't mean they're the same thing. Is a gallon of milk the same thing as a gallon of blood?"

"It doesn't say anything here about 56K, is that all right? What's a megabyte and why all this talk about blood? Have you been playing those games again? How many times have I told you . . ."

Josh's brother Trevor witnessed the scene and said, "It was pretty sad, really. When I heard him start to explain 56K, it was like watching someone try to explain quantum physics to a goat. At that point, though, he had no choice. It was like the *Titanic* after the iceberg, just a matter of time until the people started screaming."

Google

Geek Cred: The most widely used search engine on the Internet, known for its spartan design and speedy results. It creates advertising that isn't annoying and its motto is "Don't be evil." Founders Sergey Brin and Larry Page saw their company grow and grow until in 2004 it went public with the stock symbol GOOG.

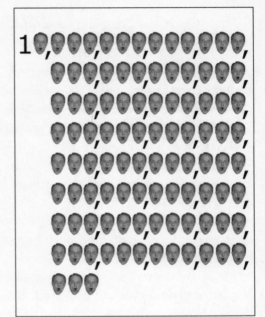

Geek Facts:

- Google removed the "Beta" label from its search engine in September 1999.

- The name Google comes from the word "googol," which is the number one with one hundred zeroes after it.

- To the surprise of most people, Google's server farm is comprised entirely of Commodore Vic-20s.

- Google knows where you are, knows what you're wearing, and knows you're reading this book. Stop slouching.

- Google's original motto was "Don't be evil to puppies, because puppies are real cute and I just love puppies, especially baby bulldogs." The reference to puppies was dropped in 2001.

- Not only do you have to be a vegetarian to work at Google, you have to be able to recite pi to one thousand places as well.

Google Acquires Gun Company Just to Screw with People's Heads

MOUNTAIN VIEW, CA – Google announced that its purchase of custom gun manufacturer Shootco Rifles was done just to screw with people's heads.

"We wanted to see what conspiracy theories people could come up with. Sparking creativity like that could turn out some great ideas, but really, it was just for kicks and giggles," said Google spokesperson Pamela Epley. "We've got lots of cash in the bank. Who can blame us if we want to have some fun?"

Before Monday's announcement, bloggers, rumor sites, and members of the media had proposed hundreds of theories. One site thought Google was building up a private militia to deal with click-fraud. Another thought the acquisition was for a hostile takeover of Honduras.

Wayne Rahman of OfficialGoogleRumors.com said, "The best theory we had was that Google would combine Google Maps with its gun company to create some sort of assassination service. It's a shame. I thought Gungle would've been a great name."

Google employees had a great time reading all the conspiracy theories. "I never laughed so hard in my life. It was the best ten million this company ever spent," said Google programmer Veronica Sands. "We should buy a condom company next."

Honduran President Maduro said he was "relieved" at the news.

Wikipedia

Geek Cred: Wikipedia is a collaborative Web-based encyclopedia that's powered by geeks. Jimmy Wales and Larry Sanger cofounded Wikipedia, though some controversy surrounds the subject. Often, battles can break out in controversial topics. However, vandalism of articles is usually quickly corrected.

Geek Facts:

- Wikipedia ran on a single server until 2004.

- Stephen Colbert encouraged vandalism of the Wikipedia entry for "elephant," asking viewers to change the entry to show that the elephant population had tripled.

- The origins of the name "Wikipedia" comes from the song "Jam On It" by the rap group Newcleus, in which some aliens sing "Wiki-wiki-wiki-wiki."

- A big fan of the English monarchy, Jimmy Wales has often considered changing his first name to "Princeof."

- The most prolific celebrity Wikipedia editor, with contributions to over three thousand articles from botany to Zaxxon, is actress Lindsay Lohan.

- Despite its geeky origins, Wikipedia's most viewed article is on Ewok orgies.

University of Michigan to Replace Libraries with Wikipedia

ANN ARBOR, MI – Facing rising costs and less state aid, the University of Michigan announced that it would be closing all its libraries and replacing them with Wikipedia.

University president Mary Sue Coleman said, "Maintaining the buildings costs millions of dollars a year, not to mention the costs of librarians. By replacing them with computer terminals connected to Wikipedia, we can use those resources to better serve the students in other ways, like free iPods."

Tom Groken, director of libraries at the university, said, "Most students use the library for research, and most do their research on Wikipedia, so why bother with books anymore?"

Students agree. "I didn't even know the library had books," said freshman Teresa Tellmore. "I just go there to study and hang out."

Critics argue that books still have their place in a university setting, and that the veracity of many Wikipedia articles is questionable. Bob Hopkins from the Kids Need to Read Books and Stop Using the Internet Foundation said, "Sure, Wikipedia is great if you need information on *Dragonball Z,* but that's hardly what students are studying in college."

President Coleman defended the action. "We have a graduate-level program in *Dragonball Z,* thank you very much."

Other colleges, such as Northwestern University, UCLA, and Princeton, are watching the Michigan program closely, and plan to follow suit if it's successful.

Craig's List

Geek Cred: When geeks need anything, they turn to Craig's List, the online classified site started by coder Craig Newmark in 1995. First, it was used to announce local events in the San Francisco Bay area, but has quickly grown to one of the largest sites on the Internet.

Geek Facts:

- Craig's List started as a simple cc email list in San Francisco.
- Ebay owns 25 percent of Craig's List, which it purchased from a former employee.
- More kidney transplants are arranged through Craig's List than through any United States hospital.
- Despite its millions of users each month, Craig's List's frugal design allows it to continue running on three iMacs.
- A recent study showed that no person under the age of twenty-seven has run a classified ad in a newspaper since the launching of Craig's List.
- At a conference for newspaper executives in 2005, a group of CEOs mooned the camera and sent the picture to Craig.

Craig's List Premium Account Features
Flash Interface, Better Ads

SAN FRANCISCO, CA – Craig's List, the popular online classified ad site, announced it would begin offering premium accounts that would give users access to a Flash interface as well as filtered ads.

"For $25 a month, users can receive an 'updated for the twenty-first century' user interface as well as have editors go through the ads and select only the best to display. We'll filter out the all-caps ads and ads that are completely stupid. Sure, we have the Best of Craig's List section, but this is customized for the individual user," said CEO Jim Buckmaster.

"We understand that some of our users are happy with a colorless and bland approach to design," said Buckmaster. "We want to give the users that aren't happy an option."

According to company research, a flashier interface is the most requested feature on the site. "Text only gives you some advantages for speed, but can anybody tell me the superhero's name that ran really fast? That's right, The Flash," said Buckmaster. "We've converted all the text into Flash. It looks really pretty. After a user enters an ad, our text-to-Flash converter takes the ad and creates a duplicate ad in Flash for premium users."

Craig's List is a private company, but it's assumed the Premium user accounts will generate more revenue. Company officials assured the press that it has nothing to do with an ad placed by owner and founder Craig Newmark, who is looking to buy a used Space Shuttle.

RIAA and MPAA

Geek Cred: If there were an Evil Empire contest for geeks, the RIAA (Recording Industry Association of America) and the MPAA (Motion Picture Association of America) would be in the final four. While there is a problem with piracy, most geeks feel that the organizations go too far in protecting their copyrights. These groups benefit the large corporations they represent while screwing most artists.

Geek Facts:

- The RIAA represents companies that produce 90 percent of the sound recordings sold in the United States.

- In addition to battling movie piracy, the MPAA also administers film ratings.

- In 2003 the MPAA decided to thwart piracy by making all movies suck. The "Cutting Off Your Nose" plan, as it was called, was abandoned in 2005.

- The RIAA lobbied to get background checks on CD-RW buyers, saying that most purchasers of those products were using them for illegal purposes.

- The RIAA projects that by 2015 its members will no longer produce any music, but will generate revenue entirely from suing file sharers.

- The MPAA proposed rating of WTF, meaning "Way Too Foreign," was rejected by executive board by a vote of 5 to 4.

MPAA Lobbying for Home Theater Regulations

LOS ANGELES, CA – The MPAA is lobbying Congress to push through a new bill that would make unauthorized home theaters illegal. The group feels that all theaters should be sanctioned, whether they be commercial settings or at home.

MPAA head Dan Glickman said this needs to be regulated before things start getting out of control. "We didn't act early enough with the online sharing of our copyrighted content. This time we're not making the same mistake. We have a right to know what's showing in a theater."

The bill would require that any future hardware will contain technology that tells the MPAA what is being shown and details on the audience. The data would be gathered using motion sensors and biometric technology.

The MPAA defines a home theater as any home with a television larger than 29" with stereo sound and at least two comfortable chairs, couch, or futon. Anyone with a home theater would need to pay a $50 registration fee with the MPAA or face fines up to $500,000 per movie shown.

"Just because you buy a DVD to watch at home doesn't give you the right to invite friends over to watch it, too. That's a violation of copyright and denies us the revenue that would be generated from DVD sales to your friends," said Glickman. "Ideally we expect each viewer to have their own copy of the DVD, but we realize that isn't always feasible. The registration fee is a fair compromise."

The bill also stipulates that any existing home theaters be retrofitted with the technology or the owner can be responsible for directly informing the MPAA and receiving approval before each viewing.

Wil Wheaton

Geek Cred: The multi-talented Wheaton could've gone under the TV, gaming, or movies categories, but the Internet category suits the modern Wil best. Wil played the precocious Wesley Crusher on *Star Trek: The Next Generation.* After jumping ship, Wil did some programming in Kansas, then reemerged on the Internet as a writer.

Geek Facts:

- He also did voice work for the *Grand Theft Auto: San Andreas* video game and the *Teen Titans* cartoon series.

- Newsgroups were created to proclaim their hatred for Wesley Crusher. One such group is alt.wesley.crusher.die.die.die.

- Wheaton turned down the role of George Costanza on *Seinfeld,* saying the role "was a dead-end job."

- Wil wrestled Jimmy Kimmel in a steel-cage match at Wrestlemania 20 and won.

- Wil has a giant tattoo of Tux the Penguin giving Bill Gates the finger on his back, and will show it to you if you ask politely.

- Wil hasn't given up the dream of being a professional dancer, the kind that dances for money, you know, a male stripper.

Wil Wheaton Implicated in Robot Fighting Ring

LOS ANGELES, CA – Actor and Internet personality Wil Wheaton has been indicted by federal prosecutors on charges of promoting and hosting a robot fighting ring.

Prosecutors allege Wheaton kicked and electrocuted as many as fifteen robots that weren't performing well. "He just blew their circuits," said U.S. Attorney Bob Schrumpkin.

Wheaton contends that nobody gets hurt in robot fighting, and that people just don't understand. "It's deeply engrained in the geek culture. We see nothing wrong with it," said Wheaton. "We get together, drink a few Red Bulls, and watch the robots fight it out. I don't see what the big deal is."

Violet Tamagotchi, President of People for the Ethical Treatment of Robots (PETR), picketed outside Wheaton's home. She doesn't buy the "part of our culture" argument. "Asimov said robots can't hurt us, so why does Wheaton hurt robots? I thought Wil embraced technology, not destroyed it," she said.

Many openly wondered if Wheaton would ever act again. "I don't know, when people see how geeky this is, they might not believe him in a nonnerd role. That could ruin him," said Chip Scoop from the *Hollywood Reporter.*

If convicted, Wheaton could face twenty-five years in prison or meet the "Electricator" fighting robot in a human-robot death match.

Jonathan Coulton

Geek Cred: With songs like "Code Monkey," "Mandelbrot Set," and "Skullcrusher Mountain," Jonathan Coulton's geek credentials can't be questioned. How else could he get a job as *Popular Science*'s Contributing Troubadour? Jonathan releases his songs DRM-free on his Web site, many at no cost.

Geek Facts:

- Coulton's folk cover of Sir Mix-a-Lot's "Baby Got Back" gained wide notoriety on the Internet.

- For one year from September 2005, Coulton released one new song every week as part of his "Thing a Week" creativity experiment.

- Not only is Jonathan Coulton geeky like his songs, but he's also half-robot.

- Coulton believes strongly in freedom, which is why he releases his songs under the Creative Commons license, and why he's been named musical ambassador to Iraq by the United Nations.

- Trimmings from Coulton's beard are highly prized in China as an aphrodisiac.

- He served as an understudy to Eric Clapton, and took Clapton's place when Eric fell ill on his last concert tour.

Jonathan Coulton or Michael Bolton?

Can you tell which of these songs are by geek singer Jonathan Coulton and which is by Michael Bolton (the singer, not the guy from *Office Space*)?

1.	"I'm Not Made of Steel"	Coulton or Bolton
2.	"Todd the T1000"	Coulton or Bolton
3.	"Steel Bars"	Coulton or Bolton
4.	"Someone Is Crazy"	Coulton or Bolton
5.	"Everybody's Crazy"	Coulton or Bolton
6.	"Can I Touch You . . . There?"	Coulton or Bolton
7.	"The Town Crotch"	Coulton or Bolton
8.	"Soft Rocked by Me"	Coulton or Bolton
9.	"Fighting for My Life"	Coulton or Bolton
10.	"Said I Loved You . . . but I Lied"	Coulton or Bolton
11.	"You Ruined Everything"	Coulton or Bolton
12.	"Drinking with You"	Coulton or Bolton

EFF

Geek Cred: Mitch Kapor, John Gilmore, and John Perry Barlow founded the Electronic Frontier Foundation in July 1990. They created the organization to defend freedoms on the Internet and in other technology realms. The EFF has been lobbying for better technology legislation and defending geeks and regular people against abuses.

Geek Facts:

- ■ The EFF got its initial funding from Mitch Kapor (designer of Lotus 1-2-3), Steve Wozniak, and an anonymous donor.

- ■ EFF was instrumental in holding Sony BMG responsible for the rootkit scandal in which CDs from Sony BMG installed rootkits on people's computers.

- ■ Because of the EFF's victory in the RIAA vs. Pianos case, Elton John and Billy Joel were able to stage their "Face to Face" tour.

- ■ The EFF successfully defended the "Hummers" from the RIAA, and kept it legal for people to hum songs in public.

- ■ The name EFF was chosen because it converts to 3839 in decimal, which is the number of times the RIAA had filed frivolous lawsuits in July 1990.

- ■ The most high-profile case for the EFF was Godzilla vs. the U.S. Army. The EFF defended Godzilla's right to privacy in email communications with Gamera.

RIAA Reanimating Dead Musicians to Eat Brains of File Sharers

LOS ANGELES, CA – The RIAA has withdrawn all the legal complaints against file sharers, and instead has decided to reanimate dead musicians, such as rapper Tupac Shakur and Johnny Cash, to eat the brains of music pirates.

"We've settled several lawsuits, but found that even after the highly publicized settlements music piracy hasn't abated. We think that a few file sharers having their brains eaten by a zombie Janis Joplin or Kurt Cobain would be more effective and create a better image than lawsuits," said RIAA chief counsel Craig Fitzsimmons.

Sandy Freshwasser from Peoria, who has over 789 GB of illegal MP3 files, said, "Isn't the RIAA supposed to be looking out for the artists? Here they are bringing them back from the dead and probably only paying them twenty cents for every brain they eat."

The RIAA had approached several living artists about eating the brains of file sharers, but most were opposed to the idea. "That's when we remembered the 'reanimation clause' that's been in every music contract since 1952, so everything we're doing is perfectly legal," said Fitzsimmons.

The RIAA can expect a legal fight from the Electronic Frontier Foundation (EFF). "We realize that the DMCA gives the RIAA the power to eat the brains of file sharers without the issue of a warrant or subpoena, but we think the law is wrong and we're lobbying to have it repealed," said EFF spokesperson Francine Parker. "We could end up with a case where an innocent person is swarmed by the undead members of Lynyrd Skynyrd, if this law isn't changed."

However, not everyone outside the RIAA was disgusted by the news. Many fans were excited by the possibility of a zombie Elvis or John Lennon visiting their home, even if it meant that they would be killed. "Do you think this means that The Dead could get back together and tour again?" gushed one fan.

QUIZ ANSWERS

Star Trek or *Babylon 5* Civilization?
Quiz Answers

(from page 35)

1.	First Ones	*Babylon 5*
2.	Goblyns	*Babylon 5*
3.	Horta	*Star Trek*
4.	Brakiri	*Babylon 5*
5.	Gorn	*Star Trek*
6.	Old Ones	*Star Trek*
7.	pak'ma'ra	*Babylon 5*

8.	K'normian	*Star Trek*
9.	Dachlyd	*Star Trek*
10.	Douwd	*Star Trek*
11.	Drakh	*Babylon 5*
12.	Vorlon	*Babylon 5*
13.	Vulcan	*Star Trek*

Vogon, Seuss, or Carroll?
Quiz Answers

(from page 43)

1.	plurdled	Vogon
2.	tulgey	Carroll
3.	lurgid	Vogon
4.	murky-mooshy	Seuss
5.	foonting	Vogon
6.	borogoves	Carroll
7.	spazzim	Seuss
8.	manxome	Carroll

9.	outgrabe	Carroll
10.	sneedle	Seuss
11.	hooptiously	Vogon
12.	jogg-oons	Seuss
13.	bindlewurdles	Vogon
14.	diffendoofer	Seuss
15.	gimble	Carroll

Superhero or Household Cleaner?
Quiz Answers

(from page 4B)

1.	Black Magic	Cleaner		11.	Boraxo	Cleaner
2.	Más y Menos	Superhero		12.	Elixir	Superhero
3.	Spic and Span	Cleaner		13.	Janitor in a Drum	Cleaner
4.	Electrasol	Cleaner		14.	Fantastik	Cleaner
5.	Elektra	Superhero		15.	Hot Spot	Superhero
6.	Mr. Muscle	Cleaner		16.	Swift	Superhero
7.	Mr. Clean	Cleaner		17.	Swiffer	Cleaner
8.	Red Tornado	Superhero		18.	Green Arrow	Superhero
9.	Eagle One	Cleaner		19.	Goof Off	Cleaner
10.	Boom Boom	Superhero				

Pokémon, Yu-Gi-Oh, or Drug Slang
Quiz Answers

(from page 7F)

1.	Barboach	Pokémon		10.	Whiffenpopper	Drug Slang
2.	Great White	Yu-Gi-Oh		11.	Magical Ghost	Yu-Gi-Oh
3.	Electabuz	Pokémon		12.	Nosepass	Pokémon
4.	Golden Dragon	Drug Slang		13.	Hero of the Underworld	Drug Slang
5.	Shroomish	Pokémon				
6.	Killer Needle	Yu-Gi-Oh		14.	Doma the Angel of Silence	Yu-Gi-Oh
7.	Weedle	Pokémon				
8.	Barrel Dragon	Yu-Gi-Oh		15.	Bambalacha	Drug Slang
9.	Zigzagoon	Pokémon		16.	Drooling Lizard	Yu-Gi-Oh

Star Wars Character or Hip-Hop Artist?
Quiz Answers

(from page 81)

1.	Luke Skyywalker	Hip-Hop	9.	Jasper McKnives	*Star Wars*
2.	Droopy McCool	*Star Wars*	10.	Sly Boogy	Hip-Hop
3.	Sly Moore	*Star Wars*	11.	Anchor Blue	*Star Wars*
4.	Talib Kweli	Hip-Hop	12.	Mabulu	Hip-Hop
5.	Mawhonic	*Star Wars*	13.	Mangu	Hip-Hop
6.	Boss Nass	*Star Wars*	14.	Rappertunie	*Star Wars*
7.	Obie Trice	Hip-Hop	15.	Joh Yowza	*Star Wars*
8.	Phoenix Orion	Hip-Hop	16.	Kit Fisto	*Star Wars*

Movie Robot or Programming Language?
Quiz Answers

(from page C3)

1.	Gort	Robot	9.	CHOMPS	Robot
2.	Robby	Robot	10.	M-MUMPS	Language
3.	AMOS	Language	11.	Johnny 5	Robot
4.	NEXUS-6	Robot	12.	DARYL	Robot
5.	Cecil	Language	13.	Occam	Language
6.	Guile	Language	14.	Rexx	Language
7.	Proteus	Robot	15.	Cilk	Robot
8.	Prolog	Language			

Jonathan Coulton or Michael Bolton?
Song Quiz Answers

(from page FD)

1.	"I'm Not Made of Steel"	Bolton	7.	"The Town Crotch"	Coulton
2.	"Todd the T1000"	Coulton	8.	"Soft Rocked by Me"	Coulton
3.	"Steel Bars"	Bolton	9.	"Fighting for My Life"	Bolton
4.	"Someone Is Crazy"	Coulton	10.	"Said I Loved You ... but I Lied"	Bolton
5.	"Everybody's Crazy"	Bolton	11.	"You Ruined Everything"	Coulton
6.	"Can I Touch You ... There?"	Bolton	12.	"Drinking with You"	Coulton

ACKNOWLEDGMENTS

I'd like to thank my editor, Richard Ember, for all the help he's given a book newb like me along the way, for giving me the chance to write this BBook, and for understanding the real meaning of being a geek. I want to thank Francisco Rangel, Nikolaj Borg, Scott Small, and Kris Koskelin for all their help with the BBook and site over the years. Without them this BBook would've been a much bigger challenge. Thanks to Mike for tying me up while I was in women's clothes (it's all innocent, Mom, I swear). Thanks to Robert for the MacGyver haircut. There are too many other people to single out who have helped me with the BBook and with the site, but I'll try. Thanks to Angel, Paul, Andy, Bill, Drew, Kyle, Seth, Jamie, Cam, Avi, Sir John, Mom, Dad, Jeff, Hedieh, Emily, Michael, the members of the BBoard, the frequent emailers, and the quiet lurkers everywhere. If you didn't see your name here, please don't launch a DDoS attack. I didn't forget you; your names have been embedded in secret code all over the BBook. Look hard.

CREDITS

All text by Brian Briggs except:

By Nikolaj Borg:
Microsoft Plan Movie Assistant in Media Player 12, page 2F
Valve to Focus Exclusively on Elite Gamers, page 7D
World Wide Web Consortium Announces New Features for CSS 3, page E9
By Francisco Rangel:
The Vatican Against Cloning in Programming Languages, page 15
We Didn't Stop Atari, page 28
Turing Test Proves Two-Year-Olds Not Human, page B5
By Scott Small:
MPAA Lobbying for Home Theater Regulations, page F9.

In addition, many Top 11 lists were collaborative efforts with the above funny geeks.
All photographs by Michael Webb of michaelwebbphotography.com.